TIME

JFK

HIS ENDURING LEGACY

BY
DAVID VON DREHLE

FOREWORD BY
CHRIS MATTHEWS

SWOONING FOR JFK
State troopers link arms to keep order as the candidate makes a Michigan appearance in late 1960.

CONTENTS

⌄

UNTIL THERE WAS NO MORE TIME

⌄

By CHRIS MATTHEWS

WHICH PRESIDENT DO YOU THINK SHOULD BE ADDED TO MOUNT RUSHMORE? It's such an American question. It deals not so much with a specific list of accomplishments but with something closer to our character: heroic stature. Who should be up on that mountain with Washington, Jefferson, Lincoln and especially that Rough Rider, Teddy Roosevelt?

In a national poll published in 2010, the answer came back "John F. Kennedy."

So much of that verdict, I think, is based on youth. We are still, in our eyes and hearts, a young country. People in other lands give regard to age and the wisdom assumed to come of it. We Americans prize above all the hope—indeed, the promise—we see beckoning us in early years.

Jack Kennedy died young. He never heard of the Beatles, never knew the term "Sixties." He was from the days of thin ties and dry martinis and cigarettes (or, in his case, those thin little cigars he smoked).

Even those final pictures we have of him that Friday in Dallas gleam at us today in the same Sinatra-era glamor, little changed from that frozen memory of his inauguration when he reworked a headmaster's phrase from Choate, instructing us to "ask not" what our country could do for us, but what we could do for our country.

This, more than any other fact of his life, set him apart: there was so little of it.

When he died, publishers went looking, as they do, for old pictures. But he looked so little different on the shining day of his death than he did when most of us first set eyes on him. Unlike all the other contenders for permanent high regard in our history, this courageous Naval lieutenant who proved himself in the South Pacific made presidential history in the same short span of years—the early 1960s—in which he was taken from us.

So he was young when we elected him our leader, the youngest ever, young when he was taken from us. Ah yes, the promise.

From January 1961 through November 1963: that's all he had. Just a thousand days, noted Arthur Schlesinger Jr., the historian who also said that "politics is essentially a learning profession." How does a young man mature in such a short space of time?

But don't you think he did? The mistakes of the Bay of Pigs gave way to the hard-learned principles Kennedy used to get the planet through the searing Cuban Missile Crisis. He knew whom to trust, whom to question, never losing sight of the essential mission: to prevent a nuclear war. If he tried to grab Cuba, the Soviets would move on Berlin, leaving him as the man to push the button. Every step the young American president took in those 13 days of conflict was to take himself back from that brink.

And not only that. Every step Kennedy took after that close call with Armageddon was in the same direction. The Limited Nuclear Test Ban Treaty of 1963 was the first great agreement of the Cold War, the earliest historic recognition by both the U.S. and the U.S.S.R. that another conflict like October 1962 needed to be out of the picture. It took just months for young Jack Kennedy to learn to do all that. The same man who ran for the presidency claiming a "missile gap," promising to defend Berlin with nuclear weapons, would end his life as a nuclear-age peacemaker.

FAST-TRACK EDUCATION *JFK stumbled at first but later showed a balance of strength and flexibility in dealing with the Soviet Union.*

He had the same fast-track education on civil rights. Cheered as a "moderate" on the issue before his election, he had to send federal troops to register students at Ole Miss. The governor of that state had refused to lift a hand. He had to push George Wallace from the door at the University of Alabama. And then he really got serious, declaring on national television that civil rights are "a moral issue … as old as the Scriptures and is as clear as the American Constitution."

He would be fighting to get the Civil Rights Bill through Congress until the day he was killed. You can listen to the tapes of him pressuring the thing through the Judiciary Committee, putting the heat on liberals as well as conservatives to get it done—until there was no more time.

It is not just what Jack Kennedy learned as a young president but, fortunately for us all, what dreams he brought to the office with him. Every Peace Corps volunteer, me included, knows how those two years changed our lives. We who watched will not forget, nor will our children and grandchildren, that we were a country grand enough in its ambitions to land its people on the moon.

There was "a touch of Winston Churchill" in this young American, my Republican father once told me. He carried with him that great man's love of history, his devotion to great causes, his regard for heroes. That he could inspire us so well is surely because he was inspired himself. It's that "surge of steely optimism," which author David Von Drehle recalls in this book, that so many of us remember and envy so much from our past.

Fifty years later, we try not to think about how much.

The writer is the host of Hardball with Chris Matthews *on MSNBC and author of* Jack Kennedy: Elusive Hero *(2011).*

THE RUN
FOR THE
WHITE HOUSE

∨

I N REVEALING CONTRAST TO THE GLAMOROUS, EFFORTLESS Kennedy of popular myth, JFK on the stump was a savvy and, at times, ruthless campaigner.

Well aware that much of the country distrusted almost everything about him—his New England–liberal leanings, the jarring twang of his Boston accent, his Roman Catholicism, his youth—like any good politician, Kennedy set about winning over skeptics by relying on the very gifts that generated suspicion in so many people. He charmed. He cajoled. He worked the crowds. And like a consummate performer, he generated the sort of frenzied response in his audience that his older, established rivals could only dream of.

As Norman Mailer wrote in a November 1960 magazine portrait of the candidate, Kennedy often resembled "a movie star, his coloring vivid, his manner rich, his gestures strong and quick, alive with that concentration of vitality a successful actor always seems to radiate."

The photos in this chapter, made by LIFE photographers who chronicled Kennedy's run for the White House, capture not only an enigmatic, intensely ambitious man making history, but the rare, heady charisma that transformed the quotidian grind of the campaign trail into political, and pop-culture, gold. —By Ben Cosgrove

LOCAL PLATFORM
From atop a step stool, Kennedy addresses an apparently skeptical crowd at a campaign stop in West Virginia.

YOUTH MOVEMENT
Candidate Kennedy sparks excitement on a college campus, a characteristic response during the 1960 campaign.

KENNEDY
FOR PRESIDENT

JOY IN THE STREETS
*Thrilled men and women—
but mostly women—respond
to the Kennedy charisma
at a stop in Texas.*

FAR FROM HOME
Kennedy campaigned to win in Texas, and with LBJ's help, he pulled off a narrow victory.

BIG SKY COUNTRY
John F. Kennedy arrives at an outdoor rally (along with then-congressman George McGovern, to his right) during a campaign swing through the Dakotas, Montana, Wyoming, Colorado and Utah.

INCANDESCENT SPEECH
Kennedy winds up his day
on the trail with a pitch to
urban dwellers—including
onlookers who don't have to
leave their homes—at a rally
in New York City.

GREAT EXPECTATIONS
In a capital dressed in white by fresh snow, JFK headed toward his inauguration.

CHAPTER ONE

THE KENNEDY
PROMISE

⌄

By DAVID VON DREHLE

JOHN F. KENNEDY WAS INAUGURATED IN BRILLIANT SUNSHINE ON AN ICY-CLEAR JANUARY DAY IN 1961, AND EVER SINCE, THAT BRIGHTNESS HAS BEEN SYMBOLIC OF PROMISING BEGINNINGS. MAGNIFIED AND REFRACTED BY A MANTLE OF GLITTERING SNOW,

the light accentuated the new president's youthful good looks as Kennedy delivered his ringing message about a torch passing to a new generation that would ask for nothing more than a chance to bear any burden for the cause of freedom. The departing incumbent, a gray and hunched President Dwight Eisenhower, wore the skeptical and vaguely grouchy look of a hero whose time has passed. The vanquished opponent, Vice President Richard Nixon, an antihero whose time was still unknown, sat half in shadow. Mythmakers of ancient Greece could not have invented a more potent script, which is why that day has become one of the most deeply etched scenes of America's history. But like the poet Robert Frost, who was so dazzled by the sunshine that he could not read the poem he had written for the occasion, subsequent generations have struggled to see past the luster of that symbolism into Kennedy's actual presidency, which was often stormy and dark.

The Bay of Pigs. The Berlin Wall. Mob violence in Alabama and Mississippi. The Cuban Missile Crisis. Vietnam. The 34 months of Kennedy's brutally shortened term were the tumultuous end of an earlier age and the difficult dawn of a new one—but not necessarily in all the ways that the young president could foresee in the blinding January noontime. Indeed, looking back on Kennedy's presidency half a century after he was slain in the sunshine of a late-autumn Dallas afternoon, it's striking just how little the man knew about what he was facing when he got started. Kennedy believed—or said he believed—in a "missile gap" that gave the edge in nuclear warfare to the Soviet Union. He believed, too, that the Soviet economy was outpacing the sputtering

COMMANDER IN CHIEF
In a scene with multiple foreshadowings, the inaugural parade passed by a symbol of the Cold War.

A TOUCH OF HARRY
At the inaugural luncheon, past-president Truman autographed the program for his young successor.

American engine, and that the U.S. was in danger of becoming a second-rate power. He feared that the United States was destined to be an also-ran in space exploration. He naively trusted his own capacity to separate truth from fiction in the labyrinth of deception that is Washington. And he thought the civil rights movement was a distraction from his Cold War crusade for freedom, when it was, in fact, a glowing crucible of that crusade.

In the space of very little time—historian Arthur Schlesinger Jr. famously framed the span as a thousand days—Kennedy was forced by circumstances and his own mistakes to look again at all of these assumptions and see them in a new light. All presidents must learn as they go, for there is no prior experience that fully prepares a person for the weight and breadth and frustrations of the job. Yet Kennedy had to learn more than most, and not just because he was young and relatively inexperienced. Kennedy had to learn not only a new job, but a new world to go with it. For better and for worse, he was the first president to come entirely to grips with the apocalyptic stakes of the nuclear age.

Perhaps it's fitting that he was blind to so much, because Kennedy himself was a dazzling mystery to the people he sought to lead. Few figures in history have been at once so compelling yet so enigmatic. Even people with front-row seats to his brief presidency, people who were with him every day and long into the night, found Kennedy elusive. A few years after his untimely death, two of his closest friends and companions, Kenneth O'Donnell and David Powers, collaborated on a bestselling memoir, and the title they chose says something essential about the 35th president of the United States: *"Johnny, We Hardly Knew Ye"*. His own wife professed that he was a difficult man to know. "He may be a fine politician," she once told a dinner party guest who had praised Kennedy's skill, "but do we know if he's a fine person?" How much of Kennedy was image only, and how much was reality?

His father had raised him to believe in image above all else. "Can't you get it into your head that it's not important what you really are? The only important thing is what people think you are," the mythmaker Joseph P. Kennedy preached to his children. The elder Kennedy had transformed himself from Wall Street wolf into Hollywood mogul, and from mogul to striped-pants diplomat. Likewise, the patriarch styled his large, dysfunctional family—with dad off philandering, mom gallivanting through Europe, and a daughter institutionalized, the victim of a failed involuntary lobotomy—into the happy clan of Hyannis Port. When Joe Kennedy launched the future president into politics, he promised to "sell Jack like soap flakes," and so he did, ultimately packaging one of the sickliest men ever to seek the White House into a model of youthful vigor at a time when America yearned for a fresh future.

Historians have struggled to see through Kennedy's carefully constructed image to the man, and the leader, within—and through the gauze of Camelot to the grit of the moment. What did John Kennedy believe, deep down? What sort of a leader was he? His style—the ineffable Kennedy charisma, élan and oratory—still exerts an undeniable magnetism on American hearts and minds. But what was the substance of his presidency? Was he a success, and by which measures? These remain slippery questions as biographers and essayists debate whether Kennedy was more warrior or peacemaker, more liberal or conservative, more visionary or pragmatist, more leader or led.

With the passage of time, though, it has become easier to see President Kennedy in full—not just as a picture of what might have been, but as a complex and nuanced leader in an age that he rightly, and frequently, described as "dangerous." During a meeting with Eisenhower on the day before he took the oath of office, Kennedy was shocked by the seemingly casual way in which the

A RADIANT DAY
Poet Robert Frost struggled to see in the bright sunlight, drawing an assist from LBJ.

departing president spoke of the possible use of nuclear weapons. The fact that the bomb had made conventional war between great powers unthinkable—a fact that was soon to be driven home by the terrifying near miss of the Cuban Missile Crisis—was still sinking in as the 1960s arrived. And all of world politics looked different in the glare of the hydrogen bomb. The United States was suddenly more powerful than any nation had ever been; its nuclear-tipped Polaris missiles and nuclear submarines alone were more fearsome and invulnerable than any armies gathered in the history of mankind. Yet at the same time, the nation was more exposed than ever to smaller conflicts waged as proxies for all-out war, in places like Berlin, Laos and outer space. And Vietnam.

Arguably, Kennedy's youth was an asset as he gradually wrapped his mind around the imperatives of this changing world. He carried scant baggage into the White House. In capturing the nomination, he had defeated the establishment wing of the Democratic party, the Southern wing and the liberal wing, by besting Adlai Stevenson, Lyndon Johnson and Hubert Humphrey, respectively. He represented an emergent force: the television-audience wing of American politics. His strength was his direct bond with people in their living rooms. Apart from his decision to appoint his younger brother Robert to his cabinet in the role of attorney general (a choice insisted upon by his father), Kennedy was free of prior ties and obligations as he put his government together. Secretary of State Dean Rusk was barely known to him, Secretary of the Treasury C. Douglas Dillon was an Eisenhower Republican, and Secretary of Defense Robert McNamara was the president of Ford Motor Co.—hardly a Washington hand. Kennedy was unencumbered by old ways of doing things, which allowed him to innovate as needed.

But youth was also a liability. Kennedy had scant experience as an executive and little feel for

the workings of a vast bureaucracy. Eisenhower sensed this; behind Kennedy's back he called his successor "Little Boy Blue." A master at the art of organizing large enterprises full of striving personalities, Ike tried to tell Kennedy that he would need a chief of staff and formal lines of command to help him delegate the burdens of the presidency. And we might imagine that someone whose executive experience consisted of commanding the 12-man crew of a little PT boat would welcome such advice from the executive who coordinated the Allied war against Hitler. But Kennedy had the hubris of youth, and scoffed at Eisenhower's rigid schedule of bureaucratic meetings and his preference for memos that distilled presidential decision-making to a simple yes or no. The new president disdained formality and preferred his data raw. He boasted of his ability to speed-read through reams of information and cut through dull briefings to the heart of things. Rather than sit atop a pyramid, as Eisenhower had done, Kennedy sought to be the hub of a wheel, with every spoke of the government's huge dynamo leading directly to him. Once in office, this approach quickly collapsed into the chaos of misinformation that led to the Bay of Pigs fiasco.

Perhaps the greatest asset Kennedy took into office was his cast of mind: flexible, inquiring, impatient, incisive. He was a voracious listener and a quick study. He had a knack for putting himself into the minds of his opponents, which was another of his father's lessons coming through. An ardent capitalist, Joe Kennedy nevertheless arranged for his oldest sons to study with the renowned socialist professor Harold Laski in London.

SIGNS OF CHANGE
JFK matched Ike's formal headgear that day, but notably doffed his hat to give his speech.

"They heard enough from me, and I decided they should be exposed to someone of intelligence and vitality on the other side." This capacity allowed John F. Kennedy to see the world through the eyes of Soviet premier Nikita Khrushchev during their perilous confrontations. His lack of ideology freed him to be a dealmaker behind the scenes, even as he was drawing bright lines in his speeches between the forces of freedom and the forces of tyranny.

Kennedy's nimble mind was the engine that propelled his winning wit and apparently easy charm. Like Abraham Lincoln, Franklin Roosevelt and Ronald Reagan, Kennedy used a facade of good humor to mask a reticent and largely isolated inner life. He understood what people wanted from him, and how to give them the impression that he was delivering it. He knew the value of a smile, a joke, a nod. As a result, he remained extremely well liked by the public throughout his presidency, no matter how his administration was faring. Shortly after the disastrous attempt to invade Cuba with a small army of CIA-trained exiles at the Bay of Pigs, the Gallup poll showed that Kennedy's approval rating had actually gone up. "It's just like Eisenhower," he marveled. "The worse I do, the more popular I get."

Kennedy came to understand something critically important about the presidency: Americans don't expect perfection from their leaders. A forthrightly corrected error can even raise the public's opinion of a president. What the public won't tolerate in the Oval Office is a person who gives up, runs out of ideas, seems overburdened by the job. In private, Kennedy sometimes complained (like many in the White House before him) that the job was too much for any rational human. He once told his rival Humphrey that if he had known the weight of the office, he would have let the Minnesota senator win the crucial West Virginia primary. He was only half-joking. Kennedy never let the public see that face, however. His presidency was a blizzard of ideas, and each time he stumbled, his next steps were taken with determination and verve.

This speaks to the haunting grip that Kennedy maintains on the world's imagination. To think of Kennedy is to feel that surge of steely optimism that he was always able to summon, to wish the ungrantable wish to know what further steps he might have taken, and where they might have led.

INAUGURATION DAY
The new president and First Lady leaving the Capitol on a brisk January day after he was sworn into office

THE ERA OF 1,036 DAYS

By SKYE GURNEY
and DANIEL S. LEVY

>

THE PRESIDENCY | **DAY** | **THE WORLD**

Jan. 20, 1961

Kennedy is inaugurated as the 35th president of the United States

Feb. 15, 1961
Sabena Flight 548 from New York City crashes in Brussels, killing 72, including the entire U.S. figure skating team

Feb. 21, 1961
The Beatles debut at the Cavern Club in Liverpool

Jan. 25, 1961
JFK holds the first live telecast of a presidential press conference

Feb. 22, 1961
Neil Simon's *Come Blow Your Horn* opens on Broadway

April 11, 1961
Bob Dylan makes first major New York appearance, performing at Gerde's Folk City

March 1, 1961
JFK establishes the Peace Corps with brother-in-law R. Sargent Shriver as director

April 12, 1961
Soviet astronaut Yuri Gagarin is the first man in space. Less than a month later, Alan Shepard would be the first American to get there

March 28, 1961
JFK starts the largest peacetime defense buildup

100

April 17-20, 1961
Fidel Castro's forces repel a U.S.-sponsored invasion of Cuba at the Bay of Pigs

April 29, 1961
ABC's *Wide World of Sports* program debuts

May 1, 1961
Harper Lee receives a Pulitzer Prize for *To Kill a Mockingbird*

May 4, 1961
The "Freedom Riders" leave Washington for the South

June 16, 1961
Despite KGB efforts to stop him, dancer Rudolf Nureyev defects from the Soviet Union

May 31, 1961
The president and Mrs. Kennedy arrive in Paris for a state visit; chic Jackie steals the show

July 2, 1961
Ernest Hemingway commits suicide in Ketchum, Idaho

June 3-4, 1961
In Vienna, Kennedy meets Soviet premier Nikita Khrushchev, who threatens to take over Berlin

Aug. 4, 1961
Barack Obama is born in Honolulu

Aug. 13, 1961
Construction begins on the Berlin Wall

200

Aug. 17, 1961
Albert Sabin's polio vaccine is licensed

A WHOLE NEW DANCE
Chubby Checker's "The Twist" had legs, reaching No. 1 on the charts in 1960 and again in early 1962.

THE PRESIDENCY	DAY	THE WORLD

Sept. 9, 1961
Nuclear test-ban talks are halted after the U.S.S.R. resumes testing

○ **Oct. 1, 1961**
The Yankees' Roger Maris hits his 61st home run

Sept. 23, 1961
JFK names Thurgood Marshall to Federal Appeals Court

○ **Oct. 3, 1961**
The *Dick Van Dyke Show* debuts on CBS

Oct. 5, 1961
The film *Breakfast at Tiffany's* debuts, starring Audrey Hepburn and George Peppard

Oct. 30, 1961
The Soviet Union explodes the Tsar Bomba, the most powerful weapon in history

Nov. 13, 1961
Cellist Pablo Casals performs at the White House

○ **Oct. 14, 1961**
How to Succeed in Business Without Really Trying opens on Broadway for the first of 1,417 performances

300

Nov. 22, 1961
JFK approves sending 15,000 military advisers to Vietnam

○ **Dec. 14, 1961**
Jimmy Dean's "Big Bad John" becomes the first country single to go gold

Dec. 19, 1961
Joseph P. Kennedy suffers a stroke

Jan. 5, 1962
TIME names President Kennedy its Man of the Year

○ **Jan. 13, 1962**

Chubby Checker's "The Twist" tops pop charts

○ **Feb. 20, 1962**
John Glenn becomes the first American to orbit the Earth

Jan. 25, 1962
JFK introduces his first civil rights bill to Congress

Feb. 14, 1962
Jackie gives a televised tour of the White House

400

March 2, 1962
Wilt Chamberlain sets NBA record with 100 points in a game

○ **March 26, 1962**
The Supreme Court establishes One Man One Vote rule in determining election districts

March 12–26, 1962
Jackie visits India and Pakistan

DAWN OF LATE NIGHT
On Johnny Carson's first night as host of The Tonight Show, *Groucho Marx was there to introduce him.*

| THE PRESIDENCY | DAY | THE WORLD |

April 13, 1962
To keep inflation in check, JFK forces steel companies to rescind price increases

May 7, 1962
Theodore H. White receives a Pulitzer Prize for his *Making of the President 1960*

April 29, 1962
JFK fetes 49 Nobel laureates at the White House to promote "the happy pursuit of knowledge and of peace"

May 19, 1962
The St. Louis Cardinals' Stan Musial becomes the National League's all-time hit leader with his 3,431st base hit

May 19, 1962
Marilyn Monroe sings "Happy Birthday" to JFK at Madison Square Garden

May 31, 1962
Israel executes Nazi chief Adolf Eichmann

500

July 2, 1962
Sam Walton starts his Walmart discount chain

July 9, 1962
Andy Warhol opens his first major show, which includes his Campbell's soup cans

June 25, 1962
Supreme Court rules compulsory school prayer unconstitutional

June 29–July 1, 1962
JFK and Jackie visit Mexico

Aug. 5 1962
Nelson Mandela is captured by South African police and begins his 27 years in prison

July 24, 1962
Kennedy orders federal agencies to end discrimination against women in appointments and promotions

Aug. 5, 1962
Marilyn Monroe is found dead in her Brentwood, Calif., home

Sept. 23, 1962
ABC debuts *The Jetsons*, its first program in color

Aug. 27, 1962
Congress passes the 24th Amendment, ending poll taxes, which had prevented many African Americans from voting

600

Sept. 30–Oct. 1, 1962
U.S. marshals provide escort for James Meredith, allowing him to register for classes at the University of Mississippi

Oct. 1, 1962

Johnny Carson starts hosting *The Tonight Show*

Oct. 16–28, 1962
The Cuban Missile Crisis pits the U.S. against the Soviet Union in a 13-day nuclear standoff

Nov. 6, 1962
Teddy Kennedy is elected senator in Massachusetts

Oct. 13, 1962
Peter, Paul and Mary's "If I Had a Hammer" hits the top 10

Nov. 7, 1962
Eleanor Roosevelt dies

A KENNEDY-ERA HERO
JFK loved the Bond novels, and during his term Sean Connery brought the secret agent to the screen for the first time.

| THE PRESIDENCY | DAY | THE WORLD |

Nov. 20, 1962
JFK bars racial discrimination in federally financed housing

Nov. 17, 1962
Elvis's "Return to Sender" hits No. 2

Dec. 24, 1962
Cuba releases 1,113 Bay of Pigs prisoners

Jan. 6, 1963
Mutual of Omaha's *Wild Kingdom* is unleashed on NBC

Dec. 31, 1962
North Vietnamese leader Ho Chi Minh promises to wage guerrilla war for a decade if necessary

700

Jan. 23, 1963
British intelligence officer Kim Philby defects to the U.S.S.R.

Jan. 14, 1963
Alabama's Gov. George Wallace calls for "segregation forever"

Feb. 11, 1963
Julia Child's *The French Chef* premieres

Feb. 28, 1963
JFK proposes civil rights legislation to strengthen voting rights

March 5, 1963
Singer Patsy Cline dies in a plane crash

March 12, 1963
Lee Harvey Oswald mails a $21.45 money order to a Chicago sporting-goods store to buy the rifle and telescopic sight he would later use to kill President Kennedy

March 18, 1963
U.S. Supreme Court orders states to provide free legal counsel to the poor

March 25, 1963
Johnny Cash records "Ring of Fire"

800

March 28, 1963
Alfred Hitchcock's *The Birds* premieres

March 21, 1963
Attorney General Robert Kennedy closes Alcatraz prison

May 1963
Gloria Steinem writes infamous Playboy Bunny article

April 12, 1963
Birmingham, Ala., police arrest civil rights demonstrators and jail Martin Luther King Jr.

May 8, 1963

Dr. No opens in the U.S.

June 12, 1963
NAACP leader Medgar Evers is murdered in Jackson, Miss.

June 7, 1963
The Rolling Stones release their first single, "Come On"

June 12, 1963
Cleopatra, starring Elizabeth Taylor and Richard Burton, premieres in New York

ON THE HORIZON
The Beatles were stirring mania in Britain, but their arrival in America was 11 weeks away when JFK died.

THE PRESIDENCY	DAY	THE WORLD

June 19, 1963
JFK sends the most comprehensive civil rights bill proposal to Congress

Aug. 8, 1963
Thieves make off with £2.6 million haul in Britain's Great Train Robbery

900

June 26, 1963
JFK visits West Berlin and declares, "Ich bin ein Berliner"

Aug. 23, 1963

The Beatles' "She Loves You" is released in the U.K. and goes to No. 1

June 27, 1963
JFK arrives in Ireland

July 24, 1963
During an American Legion Boys Nation trip to the White House, Bill Clinton meets JFK

Sept. 7, 1963
The Pro Football Hall of Fame is dedicated in Canton, Ohio

Sept. 18, 1963
The Patty Duke Show premieres on ABC

Aug. 28, 1963
During the March on Washington, Martin Luther King Jr. delivers his "I Have a Dream" speech

1,000

Sept. 15, 1963
A church bombing in Birmingham, Ala., kills four African American girls

Nov. 1–2, 1963
South Vietnam military overthrows the government and murders President Diem

Oct. 7, 1963
JFK signs the Nuclear Test Ban Treaty

Oct. 24, 1963
JFK signs the first major legislation to combat mental illness

Nov. 7, 1963
It's a Mad Mad Mad Mad World premieres in Hollywood

Nov. 22, 1963 JFK is assassinated in Dallas

Nov. 22, 1963
Lyndon B. Johnson is sworn in as the 36th president of the United States

Nov. 25, 1963
John F. Kennedy is buried in Arlington National Cemetery

NUCLEAR CONFRONTATION
Addressing the nation in October 1962, JFK announced the strategic blockade of Cuba.

CHAPTER TWO

NAVIGATING A DANGEROUS WORLD

∨

By DAVID VON DREHLE

"IT REALLY IS TRUE THAT FOREIGN AFFAIRS IS THE ONLY IMPORTANT ISSUE FOR A PRESIDENT TO HANDLE, ISN'T IT?" KENNEDY MUSED ONE DAY EARLY IN HIS PRESIDENCY. "I MEAN,

who gives a shit if the minimum wage is $1.15 or $1.25, in comparison to something like this?" He was speaking in the Oval Office to Richard Nixon, of all people—his once and possible future rival. Awkward, resentful, insecure, from hardscrabble California roots, Nixon was in many ways the antithesis of the elegant, self-assured New England trust-funder, and in time many writers would come to see them as the light and dark sides of American politics. In fact, these two men had much in common. They had known each other since their arrival in Washington as members of the freshman class of Congress elected in 1946. They were whip-smart opportunists who shared ambition and impatience. Nixon had been the second-youngest vice president in American history; now Kennedy was the second-youngest president. Both men knew that a rematch of their 1960 campaign was possible in 1964. (Only later did Nixon announce an ill-fated campaign for governor of California that briefly derailed his career.) But Kennedy was off to such a bad start that, as he ruefully told Nixon, "I don't know whether I'm going to be here in 1964."

Why was Nixon there? Because the White House had begged him to come. Kennedy needed his support. Few presidents have had such a stumbling debut as John F. Kennedy. "I 'feel in my bones' that President Kennedy is going to fail to produce any real leadership," British prime minister Harold Macmillan confided in his diary during the early months of the Kennedy administration. "The American press and public are beginning to feel the same," he added.

As friends and enemies around the world sized up the new president, Kennedy allowed the CIA and the U.S. military to open an assault on Cuba that he was unwilling to see to completion. A band of American-trained fighters was left stranded on a Cuban beach without air cover, to be killed or captured. In the aftermath, Kennedy looked so weak that Secretary of State Rusk boiled the work of the government down to a single task: "We must save this man!" A show of national unity was necessary. The stakes were incredibly high.

SUPREME WEAPON
In November 1963, Kennedy observed the test firing of a submarine-borne Polaris missile.

COMMUNIST REBEL AREAS
20 DECEMBER 1960

COMMUNIST
CHINA

BURMA

NORTH VIETNAM

• HANOI

LUANG PRABANG

*PLAINE
DES
JARRES*

VANG VIENG

*Gulf
of
Tonkin*

VIENTIANE

THAILAND

S. VIETNAM

LAOS

--- ROADS (SELECTED)

0 ——————— 150
MILES

CAMBODIA

THE COLD WARRIOR
Before Vietnam became the focus, Kennedy warned of the communist threat to Laos in a 1961 press conference.

Foreign policy was all that mattered, because the whole world was in flux. Two world wars in the space of a generation had combined to smash the old order imposed by colonial empires. Nationalist movements rolled over every continent: China was now ruled by Chinese leaders, India by Indians, the Congo by Congolese. The two nations that had emerged strongest from World War II, the U.S. and U.S.S.R., sought to shape this new globe in ways favorable to their own interests and beliefs. The result was a tinderbox, and each spark a potential disaster.

Kennedy had been given a tour of this terrain by Eisenhower and the departing cabinet on the eve of his inauguration, Jan. 19, 1961. In the Oval Office, the old general explained the "football"—the satchel full of nuclear launch codes that would be Kennedy's constant companion—and gave his successor a neat demonstration of the perks and powers of his new job. Picking up a phone, Eisenhower barked "Opal Drill Three!" Directing Kennedy's gaze to the French doors, Ike beamed as the sound of a helicopter rose from the distance, and in three minutes the chopper was settling onto the lawn.

"I've shown my friend here how to get out in a hurry," Eisenhower said as he ushered Kennedy into the Cabinet Room, where the outgoing department heads were waiting. Settling into the central leather chair, Eisenhower talked in the meeting about a rising crisis in the little nation of Laos, "the cork in the bottle of the Far East," as he put it. Communist-backed insurgents were gaining the upper hand against the government's undisciplined forces.

"You are going to have to put troops in Laos," Eisenhower predicted. The country wasn't important on its own terms; it was important because of where it was situated. Sharing borders and strategic rivers with China, Vietnam, Burma (now Myanmar), Cambodia and Thailand, Laos was the key that America's communist foes needed to unlock Southeast Asia and drive the U.S. out.

The rest of the meeting continued that theme: the world was full of small places fraught with large implications. West Berlin, for example, was a lonely outpost of democracy, entirely surrounded by Soviet-dominated East Germany. A rising flood of defectors was pouring into the Western sector, draining the East of its doctors, scientists, teachers and entrepreneurs. The communists could not afford to let this brain drain continue, and it would be an easy matter to end the exodus by sending Soviet tanks and infantry to seal the road from the West to Berlin. If that happened, the U.S. was pledged to retaliate with nuclear weapons if necessary.

And then there was Cuba, a Caribbean island of scant strategic significance but for the fact that it lay some 90 miles from the U.S. mainland. Intelligence officials had already briefed the president-elect about secret plans to topple Fidel Castro's pro-Soviet government, using Cuban exiles trained as guerrillas. Kennedy now asked Eisenhower whether these plans should be supported. "To the utmost," the president replied.

There were other hot spots, too: Korea, Iran, Taiwan. The U.S. was entangled in far more places than it could afford to defend with large bodies of troops. So instead of posting garrisons to every possible flash point, America shielded its interests and its allies under the inflexible umbrella of nuclear threat. Its missiles, its bombers and especially its new nuclear submarine fleet—which Eisenhower assured Kennedy was "invulnerable" to attack—gave America the power to unleash a holocaust virtually anyplace on Earth.

Kennedy understood that the constant threat of unspeakable destruction was the foundation of American foreign policy. After all, Eisenhower's first secretary of state, John Foster Dulles, had coined the term "brinkmanship" to explain the policy. In a crisis, the U.S. would force its opponents to back down by going to the brink of catastrophe without blinking.

PAPAL APPROVAL
After a meeting in the Vatican in July 1963, Pope Paul VI praised JFK for his peace efforts.

As president, Kennedy grew more confident in the superiority of U.S. arms, but also became convinced that Soviet strength had advanced to the point that made the risk of miscalculation in a nuclear standoff unthinkable. Although Kennedy had campaigned as a tough nuclear warrior, the dreadful weight of this dangerous policy persuaded him that he needed viable alternatives to the bomb.

The idea he embraced was dubbed "flexible response," a range of military and policy options, some highly secret. Flexible response appealed to Kennedy's love for spycraft, his appetite for danger, and his respect for dash and courage in other men. It meant recruiting and training elite corps of Special Forces troops, like the Army's Green Berets, to lead counterinsurgencies in places like Laos and Vietnam. It meant using spies to foster coups and, if necessary, assassinate enemy leaders. It also meant winning friends in distant lands through new programs like the Peace Corps and the Alliance for Progress. If the nuclear age spelled the end of all-out conventional wars between great powers, the U.S. must learn to fight small wars and win covert clashes by any and all means available.

Kennedy's approach was influenced by a rump caucus of military dissidents led by the retired Army chief of staff Maxwell Taylor, a vocal critic of Eisenhower's reliance on the nuclear umbrella. Taylor's 1960 manifesto, *The Uncertain Trumpet*, complained that fixed missiles aimed at the Soviet Union from Italy and Turkey were instantly obsolete, "stationary bulls-eyes" for Soviet targeting.

Taylor preferred options for lesser responses, and no one in the military had more options to offer than Edward Lansdale, a strange and handsome officer with a background in clandestine work whose tales of counterinsurgency entranced novelists and journalists on

MILITARY MINDS
The president huddled in the Cabinet Room with Gen. Maxwell Taylor and Defense Secretary Robert McNamara.

the steamy streets of Manila and Saigon. Lansdale had been at the side of the Philippine president Ramón Magsaysay as he battled communist guerrillas in the early 1950s, pioneering successful efforts to use soldiers to win the hearts and minds of peasant populations. Rigid in his anti-communism but flexible in his methods, Lansdale seemed a perfect (though ultimately unreliable) match for Kennedy, and the new president lost no time before installing him at the Pentagon.

The Bay of Pigs fiasco sprang in part from Kennedy's desire to think anew about the Cold War—mixed with his inexperience, his failure to know what he didn't know. The plan that Eisenhower handed off was half-baked at best: some 1,400 Cuban exiles, trained by the CIA, would land on a Cuban beach from unmarked boats in a surprise attack. Anti-Castro Cubans would rise up to greet the liberators, the planners predicted; or, if things went sour, the invading force would melt into nearby mountains to stir up a guerrilla insurgency. Because the invasion would not happen on his watch, Eisenhower had not been forced to answer the hard questions. How would the U.S. involvement remain secret? Would the Soviets use the invasion as a pretext to move on Berlin?

Kennedy tried to finesse these questions. Hoping to cloak the U.S. role, he insisted that the military have no overt involvement in the invasion. The landing zone was soon moved from a beach near the sheltering Escambray Mountains to the Bay of Pigs—the Bahía de Cochinos—across the island from Havana. But the thin veil of secrecy around the project was torn open by reporters at the *New York Times* and the *Miami Herald*, with the result that Castro was ready for the assault. On April 17, 1961, Cuban forces pinned the invaders on the beach. Only then did Kennedy wake up to the fact that architects of the plan were counting on him to commit American forces when the invasion failed.

"How could I have been so stupid?" Kennedy moaned as news of the disaster arrived at the White House. He had stumbled into the worst of both worlds: the invasion failed, and so did the secrecy. Everyone in the world knew that the U.S. was behind the feckless effort.

Kennedy was on a steep learning curve, as steep as any president in history. Even as the Cuba fiasco was unfolding, Laos skidded toward crisis, and Kennedy's attempt to threaten force without actually delivering on the threat led to a barely disguised failure. In space, the Soviets sent astronaut Yuri Gagarin into orbit, while the Americans were hardly able to lift Alan Shepard beyond the atmosphere in feeble reply. "A month-long series of setbacks rare in the history of the Republic," TIME summed up in May 1961. To Schlesinger, his staff historian, Kennedy joked mordantly that the history of the administration could be called "Kennedy: The Only Years."

The Bay of Pigs sent shock waves down through the Kennedy years and beyond. The exiles he abandoned turned resolutely Republican and became some of the most tenacious foes of Kennedy's Democratic party. (It was no accident that when Nixon at last became president, his dirty-tricks squad at the Watergate office complex included E. Howard Hunt, a Bay of Pigs planner, and a team of Cuban-exile burglars.) But that was all in the future. In the present, Kennedy's humiliation emboldened Khrushchev when the two leaders met for their first summit a month and a half later, on June 3, 1961. The Soviet leader was as stumpy as Kennedy was grand, and he arrived in Vienna toughened by life under Stalin, which weak men did not survive. He found Kennedy still reeling from the Cuba disaster, determined to project strength but distracted by a cascade of physical infirmities.

Sickly from childhood, John F. Kennedy was surprisingly frail by the time he reached the

White House. He took daily doses of hydrocortisone, prednisone and other steroids to combat his Addison's disease, a life-threatening malfunction of the adrenal glands. Additional steroid boosters were added to keep his energy and weight up (with the side effect of increased libido). He took medicine for anxiety, medicine to help him sleep, and medicine to calm his tender digestive system. The president took regular injections for allergies. Even his robust tan and ruddy chestnut hair, which he flaunted before his thin-haired cabinet, signaled illness. They were side effects of his poor health and long-term steroid overuse.

Like many chronically ill patients, Kennedy was a doctor-shopper. Janet Travell was his go-to source of procaine injections to relieve the debilitating pain of the degenerative bone disease eating his spine. Max Jacobson—known to Manhattan socialites as "Dr. Feelgood"—was flown to Vienna to provide shots of amphetamines. (A few months later, back in New York, Jacobson would end Mickey Mantle's quest for the single-season home run record when one of his Feelgood injections caused an infection.)

Wracked with back pain, Kennedy could hardly move as he perched on a chair opposite Khrushchev at the American embassy in Vienna. The Soviet premier took command of the conversation and, after lecturing Kennedy on the advantages of communism, eventually steered it toward the most dangerous flashpoint of all: Berlin. At the time, the city carried great symbolic weight. As the capital of Hitler's empire, it was the ultimate prize of the Allied campaign in Europe and, 16 years later, still teetered between the Soviet and American rivals. In a sense, full possession of Berlin represented final victory in the remade world.

Emboldened by Kennedy's failures, Khrushchev insisted that East Germany would absorb the entire city by the end of the year and warned Kennedy that he could not stop it without bringing on World War III. This decision was "irrevocable," Khrushchev declared, to which Kennedy replied weakly, "Then, Mr. Chairman, there will be war. It will be a cold winter."

Back in Washington, the president took stock of his position. To lose Berlin was unthinkable. After Laos and the Bay of Pigs, America's claim to global leadership would be shattered. But to defend the city with nuclear arms was also unacceptable. At such a moment, the Kennedy family genius for imagery kicked in. The task was to make Khrushchev believe that the American president was stronger than he seemed.

So Kennedy took to the airwaves to reassert the nation's commitment to defend Berlin as if it were an American city. For the second time in his young term, Kennedy asked Congress to boost military spending—twice as many Polaris-armed submarines; hundreds more missiles, each one vastly more powerful than the atomic bombs that ended World War II. In the first six months of his presidency, Kennedy sought and would receive a steep increase in the defense budget. Food and ammunition were stockpiled in Berlin, while troops and airmen in West Germany moved to high alert. At home, the president advised Americans to get serious about civil defense preparations, to build shelters and lay in supplies to increase their chances of surviving Armageddon.

As he projected this ghastly willingness, Kennedy was taken deeper and deeper into plans the U.S. military had devised for nuclear war. His heart sank as he realized the extent of the menace. A limited nuclear war was impossible. Once the U.S. crossed the nuclear threshold by detonating a warhead, the Soviets would surely respond with an overwhelming attack on the nation's remaining arsenal.

For this reason, nuclear-war planners were guided by the philosophy of use-it-or-lose-it: the first nation to strike must hit as hard as possible to blunt the enemy's response. The

Pentagon had targeted hundreds of sites in the Soviet Union, across Eastern Europe, and in communist China for good measure. In the words of National Security Adviser McGeorge Bundy, "The only plan the United States had for the use of strategic weapons was a massive, total, comprehensive, obliterating attack."

"What we are talking about is 70 million dead Americans," Kennedy snapped during one of these depressing sessions. Yet Khrushchev must be made to believe that Kennedy would take that step.

The danger rose through July as the flow of refugees from East Germany turned into a tsunami. Then, in the pre-dawn of Aug. 13, 1961, construction crews working under military guard began erecting a fence—soon to become a wall—to separate the Soviet-dominated sector from the rest of Berlin.

Although more hawkish voices demanded military action to tear down the barrier, Kennedy astutely recognized that the Berlin Wall was, all things considered, an important victory for the U.S. and its allies. The problem of Berlin had been resolved with nuclear trip-wires undisturbed. Khrushchev's decision effectively trapped Easterners inside East Germany, rather than move tanks and infantry to force the West out. Thus, the Soviet leader ended the brain drain without pushing Kennedy to the limit. More than that, the wall quickly came to be seen as a potent symbol of Western strength and communist weakness. As Kennedy would say when he visited the wall in 1963 (in his famous "Ich bin ein Berliner" speech), "Freedom has many difficulties and democracy is not perfect, but we have never had to put up a wall to keep our people in."

THE BERLIN CRISIS
In a rare exception from his no-sweat demeanor, JFK announced a response to Soviet threats.

At last, the president had a victory to balance out his defeats, though it was not an easy win for the world to understand. The lightning strike to build the wall left citizens of West Berlin near panic; Kennedy reassured them by sending Vice President Johnson and Gen. Lucius Clay, the hero of the 1948 Berlin airlift, in a show of continued American support. "This is the end of the Berlin crisis," Kennedy said confidently to a friend. It took some time for a boiling pot to simmer down, but as tensions cooled, Kennedy was proved right.

Even as he was picking his way through the problem of Berlin, however, Kennedy was moving further into the morass of Vietnam. Charles de Gaulle, the French leader whose troops had been driven from the former colony in 1954, warned Kennedy to steer clear of the slender coastal nation, with its postcard beaches, fertile deltas and cloud-wrapped mountains. Southeast Asia was "a quagmire," de Gaulle said. Eisenhower had urged him to fight in Laos instead. But Vietnam was a symbolic point on the geopolitical map that Kennedy would not ignore, and he focused from the beginning of his term on the war between the communist forces of Ho Chi Minh and the weak pro-Western regime in the south. "We have to confront them," the president said of the communists after his summit with Khrushchev. "The only place we can do that is Vietnam."

Kennedy's evolving intentions and beliefs with regard to Vietnam have been debated for decades, and perhaps will be forever, because he was killed before his strategy could ripen. He sent conflicting signals in the months before his death, when things were looking bad for American interests in Vietnam and military leaders were pressing him for a greater commitment. To some, he spoke firmly of his determination to win the ill-starred war. To others, he spoke of his desire to bring America's involvement to an end after his re-election. Vietnam is the great psychic scar of the Kennedy generation, and his role is an enduring

THE GREAT DIVIDE
On a viewing platform in West Berlin, Kennedy gazes across the newly constructed wall into communist territory.

riddle—even feeding a conspiracy theory that he was murdered to keep the war going.

What can be known for sure are the steps Kennedy actually took. Beginning in the autumn of 1961, he authorized the Green Berets' deployment to Vietnam, ostensibly as trainers for the South Vietnamese army. A few months later, near Christmas, his administration hushed up the death of a soldier who would become one of the 58,000 Americans to die in the war. In late 1961, he authorized the widespread use of chemicals such as Agent Orange to destroy crops in rural areas where peasants supported enemy guerrillas. And in 1963, his adminis-tration gave tacit support to the military coup in South Vietnam that ultimately served to drag America more deeply into the conflict.

These steps were all consistent with Kennedy's ideas about flexible response. They involved Special Forces, counterinsurgency tactics and behind-the-scenes skullduggery, and so they were of a different species than the huge deployments of combat troops ordered by Kennedy's successor, Lyndon Johnson. The towering Texan was a less subtle and harder-charging man than Kennedy, which served him well when he was corralling votes on Capitol Hill but led him astray in foreign affairs. To the endless what-if questions about Kennedy and Vietnam, perhaps the most certain thing that can be said is that whatever course Kennedy might have followed, it would not have been the same path that Johnson ultimately pursued.

Evidence of that can be seen in Kennedy's careful, nuanced handling of the most dramatic foreign policy episode of his presidency, the Cuban Missile Crisis. In Kennedy mythology, those fateful days in October 1962 are often portrayed as a straightforward battle of nerves in which Kennedy prevailed and Khrushchev blinked. History has painted a more complicated picture, however, in which Kennedy's pragmatism and flexibility, rather than his uncompro-mising steel, gave both leaders a way back from the edge of the abyss.

The crisis had roots at the Bay of Pigs, for the failed invasion did not end Kennedy's deter-mination to be rid of Fidel Castro. The island dictator was a thorn in Kennedy's side, openly training communist revolutionaries to take the revolution to their own Latin American countries. The president authorized a clandestine project, dubbed Operation Mongoose, that was intended to topple the dictator through cloak-and-dagger means. Supervised by his brother Robert and led by the quirky spook Lansdale, Mongoose hatched and attempted an array of plots ranging from sabotaging Cuban railroads and destroying sugar shipments to assassination by poisoned cigars, exploding seashells and Mafia hit men.

Khrushchev became convinced that the Kennedy brothers' Castro obsession would lead to another invasion—this time backed by the full force of the U.S. military. To prevent that, the Soviet leader began a secret deployment of nuclear missiles and anti-aircraft batteries to the island in the summer of 1962. In public, Khrushchev denied any plans to arm Cuba; inside the Kremlin, he justified this risky step as the simplest way to assure Castro's safety, and as an appropriate reply to American missiles deployed near the Soviet border in Turkey.

As American spies began reporting the arrival of thousands of Soviet troops in Cuba and told of Soviet freighters jamming Cuban harbors, Kennedy initially downplayed the possibility of an enemy buildup. But when a U-2 spy plane brought back photographic evi-dence of launch sites under construction, he realized that his showdown with Khrushchev had reached a climax.

"We have some big trouble," he told his brother during his first phone call after seeing the pictures. That was the morning of Oct. 16, 1962. The president was surprised at the brazenness of Khrushchev's move, which was coming after a series of Soviet nuclear tests, including the open-air detonation of the most powerful explosive ever constructed, the 50-megaton Tsar Bomba. There was no question in Kennedy's mind that the missiles in Cuba had to go—and fast, because once they were installed and armed, he would lose all leverage. Yet when his military advisers pressed their plans for a massive air attack on the launch sites, followed by an invasion if necessary, Kennedy held back. The Bay of Pigs had taught him to be skeptical of the military and its plans, and he didn't want to give Khrushchev an excuse to move against Berlin. He elected instead to impose a naval quarantine of Cuba, preventing the arrival of more missiles and warheads, while publicizing the spy photos to the world.

This measured step was a wise one. Caught red-handed, Khrushchev now found himself called to make his next moves under the hot glare of world opinion. He knew the truth behind the boastful Soviet propaganda—that no matter how large a bomb his scientists might build, his nuclear capability was no match for the growing U.S. arsenal.

Closer to nuclear catastrophe than the enemies had ever been before (or would ever be again), Khrushchev stepped back from the cliff's edge. He had no intention of leaving Cuba empty-handed, however. Khrushchev offered a deal: the Soviet missiles would be pulled out of Cuba in exchange for an American pledge not to overthrow Castro, plus the removal of U.S. missiles from Turkey.

And now Kennedy was on the spot. His advisers were nearly unanimous in urging him not to bargain over the missiles, and his generals pressed ahead with their plans for military action. The tension rose another excruciating notch when gunners on Cuba shot down an American U-2, while another spy plane was missing over Russia. In what was probably his finest hour as president, Kennedy refused to be backed into a corner. While others around him were enraged by the further provocation, the president tried to see the situation through the eyes of bystanders around the world. To them, respect for Cuban sovereignty was not too much to ask, nor was a swap for the missiles in Turkey an unreasonable request. "Let's not kid ourselves," Kennedy said as he pondered. "They've got a very good proposal." The Jupiter missiles in Turkey were obsolete, and the administration had been interested in scrapping them anyway. The Turks alone wanted to keep them, not as weapons but as symbols of America's commitment to defend its European allies. Was it really worth risking global destruction over a handful of outdated symbols?

Secretary of State Rusk argued that it might be—that even the appearance of using Turkey as a bargaining chip could undermine U.S. alliances around the world, as other nations lost faith in America's promises. Kennedy replied that no one would value those symbols once the bombs began bursting. "We all know how quickly everybody's courage goes when the blood starts to flow," he warned. And then he took Khrushchev's deal, with one caveat: the agreement over Turkey must remain secret. This much the pragmatic Khrushchev could understand. And the crisis passed.

Kennedy revealed himself as a mature and able president in the harrowing days of the Cuban Missile Crisis, which called on him to be nimble of mind and stalwart of heart at the same time. Surrounded by anxious, often overreacting counselors, Kennedy was, as all presidents ultimately must be, alone in bearing an awesome responsibility. Having allowed himself to be swept into failure at the Bay of Pigs, he was alert to the agendas and blind spots of his advisers and steered a course to success this time, when the stakes were even higher. Whatever else might be said of him, John F. Kennedy was a good learner.

THE LESSON AT CAMP DAVID

⌄
—

By NANCY GIBBS *and* MICHAEL DUFFY

AFTER THE DEBACLE AT THE BAY OF PIGS, THE RESPONSE AROUND THE world was blistering, the denunciation every bit as great as if JFK had openly invaded. Khrushchev called the effort "a crime which has revolted the entire world." America appeared aggressive and weak at the same time. Columnist Walter Lippmann, making his television debut, complained that all Kennedy had accomplished in his first months in office was to be a pale shadow of his predecessor. The administration, he argued, was "like the Eisenhower administration 30 years younger." In the Kennedy White House, there was no crueler taunt.

So he began the damage control, and here Kennedy wanted help from people he could hardly have imagined calling just four months earlier. He reached out to Nixon, who met with Kennedy in the Oval Office. "The atmosphere was tense," Nixon said. He recalled Kennedy pacing angrily, cursing the CIA, the Joint Chiefs, the White House staff: "I was assured by every son of a bitch I checked with—all the military experts and the CIA—that the plan would succeed." The two talked for nearly an hour. As Nixon left, he recalled, "I felt empathy for a man who had to face up to a bitter tragedy that was not entirely his fault but was nonetheless his inescapable responsibility."

Kennedy paid a call on Herbert Hoover as well, but the only meeting that mattered was the one with Eisenhower, who was maybe the only man on the planet with the power to help Kennedy put the disaster

TUTORING SESSION
Kennedy needed Ike's public support, but privately he also got a frank lecture on management technique.

behind him. The two hadn't been in touch much: Eisenhower had cabled a thanks in March for Kennedy's proposal that Congress restore his Army rank. But relations were formal and distant, until the moment came when Kennedy needed a serious second opinion.

To this point, Kennedy had never stepped foot on the grounds of Camp David, the presidential retreat established by FDR and renamed for Eisenhower's grandson. The next day, Kennedy climbed into a helicopter to make his maiden trip to the Catoctin, Maryland, mountains—where he would commune with Eisenhower, who came in from nearby Gettysburg and would show him around the place.

"You go down there and tell that little boy to be careful," one woman wired Ike from Iowa. "In fact, you'd better go and take over yourself."

Because this was no time for rookies. "Is there a possibility that if you had been president, the Bay of Pigs would have happened?" his son John asked. Eisenhower reminded him of D-Day.

"I don't run no bad invasions."

Kennedy may not have cared what Ike had to say. But he knew he at least had to appear to. If nothing else, the image of the two of them consulting would go a long way toward reassuring people that the young president was getting the advice he needed.

When Ike arrived at Camp David, Kennedy came to the helipad to meet him, and they immediately set to reviewing the facts. Kennedy struck the older man as candid and chastened. "He seemed to be very frank but also very subdued and more than a little bit bewildered," Eisenhower said later. "I quizzed him rather closely. He seemed himself at that moment."

They had a fried-chicken lunch in Aspen Cabin, then sat in the picture window, looking out over the two-hole putting green.

Kennedy ran through the whole story—the pressures he had faced, the promises he'd been made, the serial failures of intelligence, timing, transport, tactics. The general listened, and then called him on the carpet. Eisenhower pressed Kennedy on how the decision had been made, who had weighed in and how. Eisenhower's military life had taught him that talent was a necessary but not sufficient condition for success. The only way to guarantee smart decisions, Ike believed, was to bring all the responsible parties together and have them fight it out. "I do not believe in bringing them in one at a time and therefore being more impressed by the most recent one you hear," he said later. "You must get courageous men, men of strong views, and let them debate and argue with each other."

So he pressed the case: "Mr. President, before you approved this plan, did you have everybody in front of you debating the thing so you got the pros and cons yourself and then made the decision, or did you see these people one at a time?"

"Well, I did have a meeting," Kennedy said. But it was never the whole Security Council. "I just approved a plan that had been recommended by the CIA and by the Joint Chiefs of Staff. I just took their advice." But did you change the plan after the Joint Chiefs had signed off? Ike asked. Kennedy admitted to scaling back the air cover. Ike pressed him on this: Why did he change plans after the troops were already at sea?

The challenge, Kennedy reminded him, was to try to hide America's hand in the whole operation. "We thought that if it was learned that we were really doing this and not those rebels themselves, the Soviets would be very apt to cause trouble in Berlin."

That was exactly wrong, Eisenhower shot back. The men in the Kremlin admire strength, and understand coldly calculated self-interest. "If they see us show any weakness, that is when they press us the hardest. The second they see us show strength and do something on our own, that is when they are very cagey." The failure of the Bay of Pigs, Eisenhower predicted, will just embolden Khrushchev to do something that he would not otherwise do.

On that point, Eisenhower would soon be proven right.

As for concealing the U.S. role, Eisenhower was derisive. "Mr. President, how could you expect the world to believe that we had nothing to do with it? Where did these people get the ships to go from Central America to Cuba? Where did they get the weapons?"

PRESIDENTIAL SOLIDARITY *At the photo op, Eisenhower asked the nation to stand by their chief.*

And then he suggested, as he had during their pre-inauguration meetings, that success mattered more than secrecy—which was just what the CIA had assumed Kennedy would think. "I believe there is only one thing to do when you get into this kind of thing," Eisenhower said. "It must be a success." Or, of course, don't get in at all.

"Well," Kennedy replied, "I assure you that hereafter, if we get into anything like this, it is going to be a success."

Eisenhower said he would support anything that prevented the communists from strengthening their position in the Western Hemisphere. But the American people will not support a direct invasion, he warned, unless faced with extreme provocation. At no point, Eisenhower was relieved to find, did Kennedy suggest that the problem was an inherited plan gone wrong.

The two men walked the paths of the 125-acre compound and talked into the spring afternoon. The encounter ended with the all-important photo op, the show of presidential solidarity that would signal the world that even a humbled America remained united in its resolve. EISENHOWER URGES NATION TO BACK KENNEDY ON CUBA ran the front-page headline in the *New York Times*, next to the picture of them walking the paths, heads down, Ike's hands and hat clasped behind his back. "I asked President Eisenhower here to bring him up to date on recent events and get the benefit of his thoughts and experience," Kennedy said. Eisenhower dutifully declared, "I am all in favor of the United States supporting the man who has to carry the responsibility for our foreign affairs."

When it was over, Eisenhower was eager to show his pupil the grounds; he knew his way around, knew some of the personnel. The compound included a bowling alley and movie theater, an unheated pool, a skeet range, and the one- and two-room cabins Roosevelt had had built and equipped with his favorite chiming Navy clocks. He walked him down to a small cottage called Dogwood. "I want you to see what these are like," he said. Then Kennedy drove Eisenhower back to the helipad and suggested they play golf together soon.

Eisenhower had renamed Roosevelt's Shangri-La as Camp David, and it was of course Kennedy's prerogative to change the name again. Three days after the visit, the White House announced that contrary to any speculation, the official presidential retreat would continue to be known as Camp David.

TIME *editors Nancy Gibbs and Michael Duffy are the co-authors of* The Presidents Club: Inside the World's Most Exclusive Fraternity, *from which this piece is adapted.*

IMAGE OF OPPRESSION
When authorities in Birmingham, Ala., turned fire hoses on black protestors, the photos sparked outrage.

CHAPTER THREE

HESITANT WARRIOR
FOR CIVIL RIGHTS

∨

By David Von Drehle

THE 1960 PRESIDENTIAL ELECTION WAS AMONG THE CLOSEST IN HISTORY, A MATTER OF RAZOR-THIN MARGINS IN A COUPLE OF SWING STATES, AND WHEN THE NUMBERS WERE ALL TALLIED AND CERTIFIED AND ANALYZED, IT WAS NO OVERSTATEMENT TO SAY

that John F. Kennedy owed his presidency to black voters, and to their thirst for justice. Endless attention over the years has been given to the historic Kennedy-Nixon debates, the first ever televised. But another event, even later in the campaign, tipped what may have been a more critical bloc of votes.

A young civil rights leader, Martin Luther King Jr., was arrested in his hometown of Atlanta and jailed for trespassing after he tried to be seated at the whites-only restaurant in a downtown department store. Officials in nearby DeKalb County, where King was recently given a suspended sentence on a minor traffic offense, decided that King had violated the terms of that sentence and ordered the preacher to four months on a prison work gang. Given the reality of prison violence, King's wife Coretta feared that this would be a death sentence.

Neither Kennedy nor Nixon breathed a word about the outrageous injustice, for they were locked in combat for the votes of Southern whites. Then aides to Kennedy hit on the idea of having the candidate place a telephone call to Coretta Scott King, not to comment on the case but to express his sympathy and concern.

This exchange of less than two minutes had a galvanizing effect. Officials in Atlanta—which billed itself as "the city too busy to hate"—pulled strings to have King set free, and joyful blacks gathered to celebrate at the King family's Ebenezer Baptist Church. His deep voice thundering from the pulpit, King's influential father declared, "I had expected to vote against Senator Ken-

FREEDOM SUMMER
During the March on Washington, King delivered his immortal words: "I Have a Dream."

WE MARCH TOGETHER
CATHOLIC
JEWS
PROTESTANT

BANDING TOGETHER
After the peaceful march, Kennedy was emboldened to pose in the White House with King and civil rights leaders.

HOSTILE TERRITORY
The National Guard was called out to protect Freedom Riders on the road from Montgomery.

nedy because of his religion. But now he can be my president, Catholic or whatever he is. It took courage to call my daughter-in-law at a time like this." The patriarch continued: "I've got all my votes and I've got a suitcase, and I'm going to take them up there and dump them in his lap."

Soon after, on Election Day, the shift in the black vote was little remarked upon but hugely significant. According to pollster George Gallup, Kennedy carried about 70% of the black vote in 1960, a decisive improvement over Democrat Adlai Stevenson's 61% share four years earlier. This margin in the heavily black cities of Chicago and Detroit was likely enough to tip the extremely tight races in Illinois and Michigan—and give the electoral college to Kennedy.

So King and his fellow civil rights leaders were understandably dismayed to find President Kennedy timid and selfish on racial issues at the outset of his term. Though he appointed a progressive lawyer, Harris Wofford, to be his liaison to the movement, Kennedy seemed determined to keep Wofford at arm's length. And the president's dealings with King himself were kept hidden from the press.

The first of these encounters during his presidency occurred, by coincidence, on the day after the Bay of Pigs—the same day Kennedy commiserated with Nixon over foreign affairs. King met that day with Robert Kennedy and his civil rights staff in secret at the Mayflower Hotel. Afterward, Wofford took King to the White House nearby. As planned, the president "accidentally" found King when he poked his head into Wofford's office, and the two men exchanged a few words. "If you ever need me, you know the door is always open to you," Kennedy said—but evidently not the front door, where everyone could see.

The day quickly arrived when civil rights leaders did need Kennedy. On May 15, 1961, about a month after his furtive encounter with King, Kennedy woke to find a front-page story in the *New York Times*: BI-RACIAL BUSES ATTACKED, the headline trumpeted. In the unsettled aftermath of the botched Cuba invasion, no one had warned the president that a group of white and black students had volunteered to ride public buses across the Deep South to challenge unconstitutional state laws segregating public facilities for interstate travelers. They called themselves the Freedom Riders. Near Anniston, Ala., a mob managed to stop one of the buses and burn it by the side of the road. When a second bus made it to the Birmingham station, the exiting passengers were brutalized by rioting whites armed with bats, fists and chains.

The president was furious—at the protesters. "Can't you get your goddamned friends off those buses? Stop them!" he scolded Wofford. On a personal level, Kennedy disapproved of segregation, and as a matter of law he knew that the Freedom Riders were right. But he thought they were moving too quickly and groused that the violence they invited was a propaganda boon to the Soviets.

Robert Kennedy's weak response was to dispatch his lone Southern-born aide, a former newspaper reporter from Nashville named John Seigenthaler, to speak with the injured Riders and seek help from the Alabama governor. But by the time Seigenthaler reached Birmingham, more students were arriving to pick up the torch—much as President Kennedy had urged them to do in his ringing inaugural message. Rather than let Seigenthaler talk them out of their mission, they quoted Kennedy's words. They were part of that new generation paying the price for freedom.

Kennedy heard similar words in Washington. In one telling exchange with the black newspaper publisher and influential Democrat Louis Martin, Kennedy seemed puzzled when Martin told him that "Negroes are getting ideas they didn't have before," ideas of hope and aspiration. "Where are they getting them?" Kennedy asked. "From you!" Martin replied.

Seigenthaler was at the Montgomery, Ala., bus terminal when the next leg of relay arrived from Birmingham. Another mob lay in wait. In the storm of violence that followed, the Kennedy representative tried to rescue two young women under attack; Seigenthaler was beaten so badly he required hospitalization. Later, a larger mob surrounded Montgomery's First Baptist Church, where King and other civil rights leaders were trapped with a group of 1,500 people. Only when the mob threatened to attack the building with the crowd inside did Robert Kennedy order a makeshift army of U.S. marshals to the scene. President Kennedy said little in public—only a brief, tepid statement.

What explains Kennedy's lack of leadership? Like others before him, he felt boxed in by the strange history of his Democratic party. Shattered a century earlier by Southern secession and the Civil War, Democrats reconstituted themselves as an uneasy partnership of cosmopolitan progressives, blue-collar ethnic voters, and Jim Crow segregationists in the South. Kennedy was constantly under pressure from both ends of this difficult coalition. His legislative agenda could never pass Congress if the sizeable bloc of Southern votes abandoned him. Given his Massachusetts heritage and his Roman Catholic faith, he was already on thin ice with Dixie. (In 1960, Virginia's Harry F. Byrd and South Carolina's Strom Thurmond, signers of the pro-segregation "Southern Manifesto," received more electoral votes in Mississippi and Alabama than Kennedy did—and they weren't even on the formal ballot.)

The judges of the federal Fifth Circuit Court of Appeals were not so troubled. Led by a group of courageous anti-segregationists known as "The Four," the Fifth Circuit kept up relentless pressure for change in the Southern states. To Kennedy fell the duty to enforce these rulings, whether he wanted to or not, as Southern voters stiffened their backs and thumbed their noses by electing ever more strident foes of equal rights. In 1962, Alabama voters elected

SHOW OF FORCE
Before Robert Kennedy sent out armed guards, mobs viciously attacked Freedom Riders on their buses.

George Wallace as governor, and he repaid their votes by promising in his inaugural address: "Segregation now, segregation tomorrow and segregation forever!"

This showdown turned deadly in the autumn of 1962, after the Fifth Circuit insisted that the University of Mississippi admit its first black student, James Meredith. Again, the president kept his distance, handing the problem to his younger brother. Department of Justice lawyers searched for a deal behind the scenes that would allow Gov. Ross Barnett to say that he had done his best against the federal intrusion, then step aside to let Meredith pass. But Barnett pushed too hard. He demanded that U.S. marshals actually force their way into the registrar's office at gunpoint. Informed of the proposal, President Kennedy demurred, worried about provoking violence. Instead he took a page from Eisenhower's handling of the Little Rock desegregation crisis of 1957 and readied federal troops in case of trouble.

And trouble came. After Meredith arrived at the university, Barnett withdrew the state troopers from the Oxford campus, leaving a few hundred lightly armed federal marshals to face a mob of a thousand, chanting: "Go to hell, JFK!" Protesters grabbed bricks, bottles and pipes, and some pulled guns. Reluctantly, an official on the scene authorized tear gas, but it did little good. The riot continued through the night, leaving two dead and more injured. Only the arrival of federal troops near dawn—some eight hours after the violence broke out—put an end to the melee.

A reporter for the Scripps-Howard newspaper chain was appalled by the lack of leadership; both the governor and the president had failed, and their failure opened the door to disaster. "All the state hoped to accomplish by continued resistance was to compel President Kennedy to order in troops," wrote Richard Starnes. "And the White House ... sought at all costs to avoid use of troops [because] it would be a political liability all over the South." Starnes closed on a note of disgust: "Was the tragedy of Ole Miss caused by nothing more than ordinary, squalid courthouse gang political haggling?"

LINGERING TABOO
Kennedy was afraid to be seen with interracial couple Sammy Davis Jr. and his wife May Britt.

To Kennedy's relief, however, Northern voters rallied to support the president. Whether the troops arrived promptly or late seemed to make little difference. Pollster Lou Harris reported widespread approval of Kennedy's "firm and resolute leadership" in the Mississippi crisis and urged Democrats running for Congress to put the issue "front and center." The African American vote swung still further into Kennedy's column, up from some 70% in 1960 to nearly 85 % now—a clear sign that the Democratic party was moving into a new era as the home of minority voters.

Yet he persisted in scolding the civil rights movement. "You're making my life difficult," Kennedy told John Hannah of the U.S. Civil Rights Commission when Hannah proposed a series of public hearings on discrimination. "I would appreciate it if you didn't." Despairing over the president's back-door approach to racial justice, Wofford sprang at a chance to leave the White House in favor of an assignment in Africa with the fledgling Peace Corps. Jacqueline Kennedy left a White House reception in tears because her husband refused to be photographed with performer Sammy Davis Jr. and his wife May Britt, a white woman from Sweden. "Get them out of here," he hissed to an aide when he saw the interracial couple.

Martin Luther King Jr. grew so frustrated with white leaders like Kennedy—self-styled moderates who urged blacks to "go slow"—that he singled them out in his famous "Letter from Birmingham City Jail," dated April 16, 1963. His most perplexing foe, he declared, was not the outright bigot but the middle-of-the-roader. "I have almost reached the regrettable conclusion that the Negro's great stumbling block in his stride toward freedom is not the White Citizen's Counciler or the Ku Klux Klanner, but the white moderate, who is more devoted to 'order' than

to justice; who prefers a negative peace which is the absence of tension to a positive peace which is the presence of justice; who constantly says: 'I agree with you in the goal you seek, but I cannot agree with your methods,'" he wrote. "Lukewarm acceptance is much more bewildering than outright rejection." King's brilliant indictment was soon followed by televised scenes of Birmingham police attacking black children with fire hoses and snarling, snapping dogs. Then Alabama's banty Gov. Wallace vowed to stand in the doorway at the University of Alabama to prevent court-ordered integration. And at last, President Kennedy reached the conclusion that he must step up and lead, rather than continue trying to hold the movement back.

On June 11, 1963, after National Guardsmen had escorted the students past Wallace and into the Alabama campus, Kennedy took to his favorite forum—a live television address from the Oval Office—to tell Americans that "we face … a moral crisis as a country and as a people.

"I hope that every American, regardless of where he lives, will stop and examine his conscience" about the question of equality. "Today," he said, "we are committed to a worldwide struggle to promote and protect the rights of all who wish to be free. And when Americans are sent to Vietnam or West Berlin, we do not ask for whites only. It ought to be possible, therefore, for American students of any color to attend any public institution they select without having to be backed up by troops." And it ought to be possible for any citizen to choose a hotel room or eat in a restaurant, and to cast a vote without fear.

After more than two years of temporizing and dodging, Kennedy finally proposed the historic legislation that Congress eventually passed after his death,

MARTYR'S DAY
The president met with Medgar Evers's widow, children and brother in the Oval Office.

laws that would reshape the U.S.: the Civil Rights Act of 1964 and the Voting Rights Act of 1965. For the first time since the failure of Reconstruction nearly a century before, the federal government took a bold stand for equal rights.

But the president closed his speech with an important insight: "Legislation, I repeat, cannot solve this problem alone. It must be solved in the homes of every American in every community across our country." Hatred festered in hearts, not just in laws—and as if to prove the point, civil rights leader Medgar Evers was murdered in his driveway in Jackson, Miss., that same night, shot in the back by a man who would go free for more than 30 years.

Even now, Kennedy remained wary of Martin Luther King Jr. Perhaps he understood that King was a rival for the gaze of history, a man even younger and more compelling and more eloquent than Kennedy himself, a man of such force that he didn't need the presidency to change the world. That sort of person can unnerve any president. When King and other movement leaders called for a great March on Washington in August 1963, Kennedy agreed to a public meeting with the organizers, but only after the event was over, so that he could cancel and avoid King should things go badly. The day was a huge success, of course; more than a quarter-million peaceful citizens in the blazing sun, swaying to the gospel cries of the immortal Mahalia Jackson, who opened for King and urged him to put his prepared remarks aside. "Tell them about your dream, Martin," she called to him—and he did.

Kennedy's broad smile when he posed afterward with King and the others for an official photograph serves to document how much had changed for this too-timid president. And though the racial violence would deepen—four young girls were killed in a Birmingham church bombing a few weeks after the Oval Office meeting—no longer would a hero have to enter the White House in secret, simply because of the color of his skin.

A SEA CHANGE IN STYLE

⌄

When the Kennedys moved into the White House, the difference was dazzling, as the late TIME *columnist Hugh Sidey reported in his 1963 book,* John F. Kennedy, President. *An excerpt:*

By HUGH SIDEY

THE COUNTRY HAD INSTALLED ITS new president with a flourish. It liked his style and his words. Now the nation would wait a bit to see what he could do. In the meantime the people studied the man, his wife and his children. Every move was written about. Every word recorded. After the Kennedys had the new administration appointees over for a Sunday night reception, the Washington society columnists gasped. The *Evening Star*'s Betty Beale listed eight social precedents that were shattered in the single evening.

By far the biggest headlines went to the fact that there was an honest-to-goodness bar that dispensed hard liquor right out in the open. It

ICON OF COOL
JFK's style trademarks were all about classic sportiness: sunglasses, slim suits, khakis and polo shirts.

was no secret that in previous administrations you could get a little bourbon or maybe even a martini if you knew how to go about it, but never in recent years had the cocktail been given such status. There were ashtrays scattered about, too, which meant that smoking was allowed, another break with tradition. "Naturalness was the keynote of this party," sighed Miss Beale, still shaken by the new look when she got to her typewriter. Children had been invited also, and they romped among the grownups. Fires burned in the fireplaces, and small bowls of blossoms decorated the niches and tables.

Still at her typewriter, Miss Beale figured it out: "But obviously, President and Mrs. Kennedy have decided that they are going to offer the same hospitality to their guests when reporters are present as they would naturally do if they weren't, or if they were living back in their own house on N Street."

"The reason for this reception," Kennedy told his guests, "is the desire to see some of the names I have been reading about in the newspaper."

The long hours of the days were filled with work: wearying meetings, thick reports to be read and acted upon. Though so much of the Kennedy life was and is work, the critics of this phenomenal American family sometimes tend to overlook the drudgery that goes into a Kennedy triumph. The writers always note that the Kennedys have money, good looks and power. To mold them into success, however, takes more than a magic word. The new president was invariably awake by 7:30 or 8 in the morning. Sometimes he read newspapers in bed as he ate breakfast; at other times he dressed for a work session while he consumed two poached eggs. Kennedy walked to his office by 8:30 or 9 and plunged into meetings. Seldom did he leave before 7 or 8 p.m., and many staffers would send papers on his telephone demand to the private quarters as late as 11 p.m. So burdensome were the frantic early days that once he looked at an aide and said, "Nixon should have won the election."

THE NAUTICAL LOOK
JFK's affinity for sailing near the compound in Hyannis Port provided some of the era's most memorable imagery.

The large Oval Office began to look and feel like President Kennedy. The pale-green walls were smothered in a coat of New England off-white. The two couches flanking the fireplace were hurried out and re-covered in a light beige. A new stock of oak firewood was rushed in for the fireplace, which now crackled all the time. There were the marks of a Navy man: on the walls flanking the fireplace hung two naval pictures showing the 1812 battle between the *Constitution* and the British frigate *Guerriere*, and on the mantle was a model of the *Constitution*.

Just before the Kennedy children and the faithful terrier Charlie flew up from Palm Beach to take up residence in their famous new house, Jackie let the public in on how she had decorated their rooms: Caroline's was painted a pale pink with white woodwork, John's white with white woodwork and blue trim around the door moldings. The information was rushed over the wires and received as much space as the heavier matters of state. Reporters pestered and Jackie reluctantly let out a menu of a dinner served to Bob and Ethel Kennedy: consommé Julienne, filet of beef, sautéed mushrooms, potato balls, mixed green salad, assorted cheese and crackers, crème brulée with strawberry sauce and coffee.

A huge snowman with button eyes and a carrot nose waited for Caroline in the backyard of the White House, the sculpture done by the gardener. She was delighted. In fact, she was fascinated by all her new surroundings. After taking a second look at the snowman with her father in tow, she toured the president's office. She got a view of the indoor swimming pool, stuck her hand into the water and exclaimed, "It's warm." And when the diplomatic corps was invited

to a reception, she helped greet the guests in a fancy party dress ("It's my very best," she told admirers). No doubt there will be many endearing sights in this administration of young people and young children, but few will top the picture of Caroline standing on the red carpeting in the foyer of the White House listening to the president's own Marine band. Her foot twitched to the music, and when she was granted a special request, she asked for "Old MacDonald Had a Farm," which was rendered with such polish that few of the diplomats noted the tune.

If Caroline was a hit at this reception, so were other Kennedys. Jackie moved slowly among the people in the huge State Dining Room, using her French often. Bob Kennedy, bumping into Soviet ambassador Mikhail Menshikov, asked him to come to the Justice Department, "where we check up on communist spies." Replied the jolly Russian, "Perhaps I'll come one day and look at the outside." When the president approached Madame Hervé Alphand, wife of the French ambassador, he greeted her in French, "Comment allez-vous?" and then laughed and lapsed into English. "My wife speaks good French. I understand only one out of every five words ... but always 'de Gaulle.' "

PRESIDENT AT PLAY

While visiting Santa Monica, JFK took to the beach. In the Oval Office, he set a beat for Caroline and John Jr.

Joe Kennedy laughed about the evening when he had talked with Caroline on the phone from Palm Beach. In the background the elder Kennedy could hear a presidential plea: "Hurry up, Caroline, I want to use the phone."

One afternoon, a presidential itch to see the movie *Spartacus* sent the Secret Service scurrying to the Warner Theater to check its safety. That evening after the lights were dimmed, Kennedy and his friend Paul B. Fay Jr., now undersecretary of the Navy, slipped in undetected. Noting a familiar figure in the row ahead of him, the president tapped Orville Freeman on the shoulder. "This is a hell of a way to write a farm program," said the grinning Kennedy to his Secretary of Agriculture. Freeman, like Kennedy, had sought out the dark theater to escape for a while from the long office hours.

His reading suddenly became a phenomenon. Reporters found that he read their every word, and sometimes called them up to praise or complain. He consumed five newspapers with his morning coffee. In voracious glances he could absorb a difficult memo on economics. He read from 1,200 to 2,000 words a minute, maybe faster when the going was light. When he

FORMAL FOOTWORK
The East Room became the scene of glittering galas. At this one, the president can be seen near the window at rear.

wanted the facts on Cuba and the rise of Castro, a massive government document was trotted out. Timidly an aide suggested that Kennedy read the synopsis, but the suggestion was halted with a Kennedy wave. He went through the detailed account.

Kennedy had a weakness for a fine phrase. One staff member insisted that the "New Frontier" began in a French phase, simply because of the eloquent message sent to Kennedy by Charles de Gaulle after the election. Kennedy sometimes wondered how much of Winston Churchill's stature was built on the use of words. Often he read the Churchill memos just to savor their craftsmanship.

Though the president generally stuck to nonfiction, he occasionally strayed. It was discovered with some relish by mystery buffs that he was a fan of the hard-drinking, hard-fighting British Secret Service agent James Bond, the creation of Ian Fleming.

Kennedy was a memo man. Soon after he took office, he ordered a dictaphone installed beside his desk. Throughout the day he would whirl and talk into the machine. Toward evening his secretary Evelyn Lincoln would rescue the transcriptions and type out the memos. They were terse messages, sometimes only a sentence or two centered on an 11-by-8 sheet of paper. There was a low key about them, like Kennedy himself. They had an understated manner, almost a politeness in "suggesting" and "appreciating" rather than demanding. In the thick sheaves of memos was the constant quest for information. "I would like to have more information on the progress of the negotiation with the Germans on increasing their participation in foreign aid to the underdeveloped countries and to defense." From the White House routine came a hint of the Kennedy administrative style. Out was the formal, board-of-directors type of management. John Kennedy lived and worked informally. He phoned people when he wanted to talk to them. He summoned them when he wanted to look at them as he talked.

Kennedy from the start took time to see reporters. And in the lull of one noon, he talked to me. He was behind his desk as I first entered, a desk littered with papers, scratch pads, books and thick memorandums. For a few precious seconds as I walked across the rug, he turned to the small table behind him on which the day's newspapers and magazines were neatly arranged. He bent his head briefly to scan the headlines, and then he whirled and put out his hand. It all seemed different now as he approached. Doubtless there was little physical change in the few short weeks of office—perhaps the tan had faded a little, the lines around the eyes were etched more finely from the constant reading. But the real difference in this meeting was in the office, which for the moment seemed to be the biggest office in the world. It was bright with its white paint, the temperature several degrees cooler than in the surrounding rooms. The sun cast diffused squares of light on the thick rug after filtering through the drapes. The surroundings were now all Kennedy. Even Eisenhower's old desk bookends—the golden eagles—were perched on the wall bookshelves. In their places were miniature shipboard cannons from Revolutionary War days.

The manners were the same. Kennedy gestured toward a chair and then sat carelessly behind his desk and clasped his hands around a knee. When the office doors are closed, the silence is enormous. The president sits only a hundred yards from bustling Pennsylvania Avenue. Beyond his office walls the antechambers bulge with secretaries and aides. But suddenly it was quiet, an unusual atmosphere for Jack Kennedy, who for four long hard years never seemed to be out of sight and sound of a huge American crowd of voters. In the quiet, Kennedy talked about his job. He chafed a bit at the thought that some of the impatient journalists were demanding accomplishment so soon. He simply had not had time to learn as much as he needed to know,

ACE ON THE LINKS

Enjoying a round in Newport, R.I., along with Jackie and Tony Bradlee, wife of Washington Post *editor Ben.*

to make the firm decisions that he realized must soon be made, to assemble the intricate programs that he had to follow. His action was still reaction. But it would change, he promised. Kennedy dwelled for a minute on the "export of the communist revolution." This was the challenge before him. "How do you combat guerrillas?" he asked. "That question must be answered." The president's mind wandered back over other crises of other years. For just a fleeting moment, he wondered out loud why we did not do more at the time of the Berlin airlift to show the Russians we meant business. There was even then a trace of presidential doubt over our ability to wage an effective war in Laos.

Kennedy remarked on the men around him. "Good men," he said. And he revealed that he had just decided to appoint John J. McCloy and Arthur H. Dean to help him with problems of disarmament and nuclear testing. Both men were tough and independent, he said, not wedded to any previous positions, and for this reason he wanted them. Suddenly the office door flew open. Aide Kenneth O'Donnell, the appointments secretary, entered, and with him came the sounds of the outside world. The words were reassuring, but all the problems remained.

ALL THE WAY WITH JFK

THE RANK AND FILE
Pitching economic stimulus, JFK spoke to the United Auto Workers convention in 1962 in Atlantic City.

CHAPTER FOUR

SEEKING THE
NEW FRONTIER

∨

By David Von Drehle

THROUGH THE IMPERFECT LENS OF MEMORY, THE LATE 1950S AND EARLY 1960S LOOK LIKE A PERIOD OF BOUNDLESS PROSPERITY: HUMMING FACTORIES, INSTANT SUBURBS, BIG FINS ON LONG CARS. BUT THE REALITY WAS SOMETHING DIFFERENT.

John F. Kennedy took office as the U.S. economy was struggling to recover from the sharp recession of 1957–58, when unemployment in the auto industry reached 20% and a dread combination of stagnant growth and rising prices rattled the confidence of the American public.

Kennedy promised to "get America moving again" with a package of initiatives that he called the New Frontier. Along with his buildup in military spending, Kennedy envisioned government health insurance for elderly Americans, federal aid to schools, more low-income housing, free trade with Europe, and more. He faced two large problems, however. The first was the federal budget deficit. Kennedy had a bone-deep skepticism about deficit spending. His determination to keep the deficit lower than it was during the Eisenhower administration left his policy aides feeling handcuffed. The second problem was Kennedy's weakness in Congress. Although Democrats controlled both the House and the Senate, many were on Kennedy's team in name only. Conservative Democrats—including large numbers from the Southern states—were almost as likely to vote with the Republicans as with their own president. Navigating the factions on Capitol Hill required skills that Kennedy and his staff did not possess; Bobby Baker, Democratic Senate majority secretary, said that Massachusetts pol Larry O'Brien, who managed Kennedy's congressional relations, had "no appreciation for the complexities of Capitol Hill." Kennedy had to learn by trial and error, suffering so many defeats in his first year as president that he groused he "couldn't get a Mother's Day resolution

BACK FROM SPACE
The president and John Glenn examined the Mercury capsule that carried the astronaut into orbit.

SIGNS OF A REBOUND
Taking office after a fierce recession, Kennedy made economic recovery one of his top priorities.

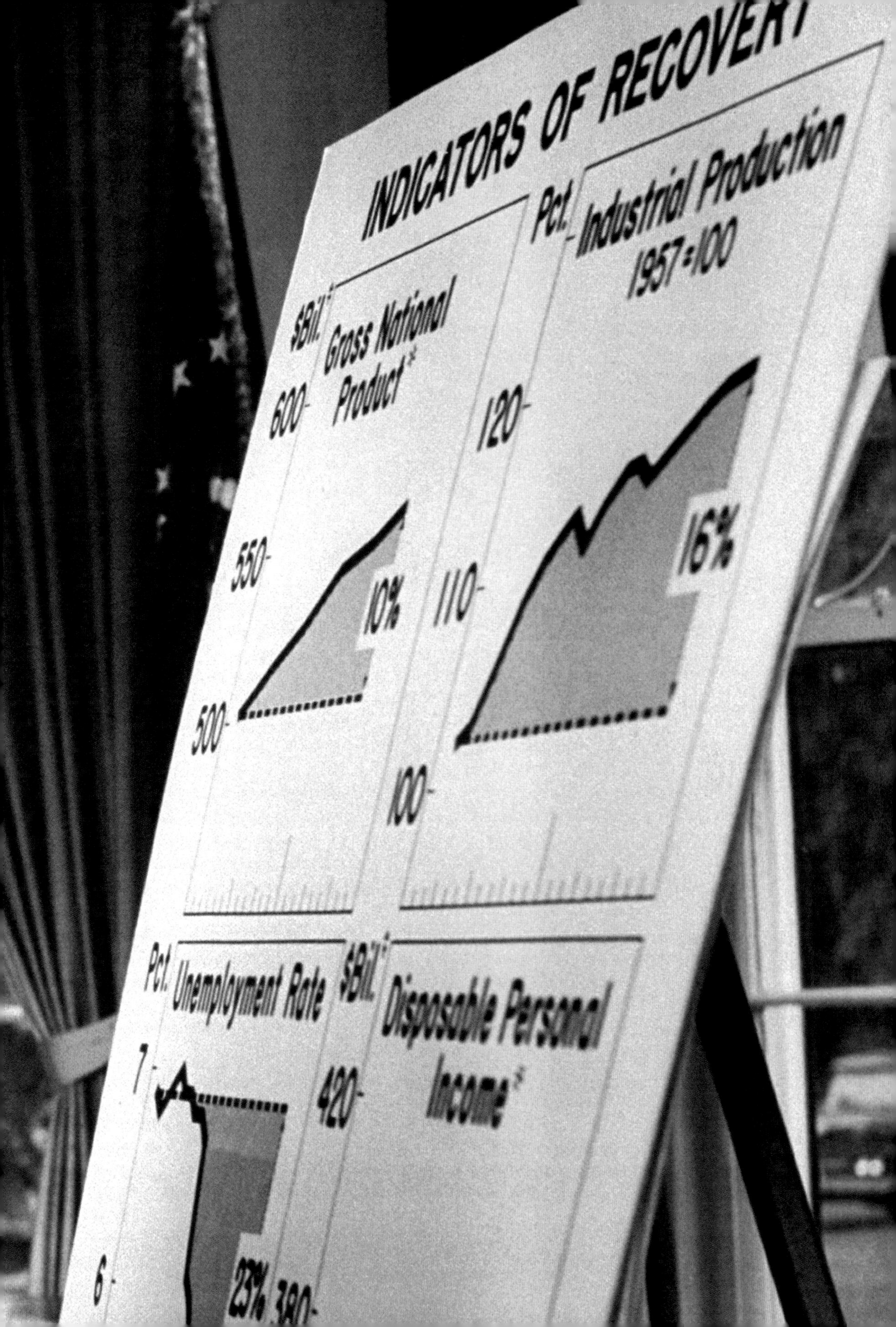

INDICATORS OF RECOVERY

$Bil. *Gross National Product* *

600—

550—

500— ·········

Pct. *Industrial Production 1957=100*

120—

110—

100—

10%

16%

Pct. *Unemployment Rate*

7— ·········

6—

23%

$Bil. *Disposable Personal Income* *

420—

390—

A MAN OF MEMOS
The president, dictating to his secretary Evelyn Lincoln, fostered a blizzard of new ideas.

through the goddamned Congress."

Strikingly, Kennedy even had trouble with his fellow Irish Catholic politicians from Massachusetts, led by Rep. John McCormack of Boston, who stepped up from majority leader to speaker of the house in 1962. McCormack clashed with the president and was joined in combat with Kennedy by his protégé, Thomas "Tip" O'Neill, the basso profundo who occupied the congressional seat that was Kennedy's a decade earlier.

Kennedy knew that his strength in Congress would grow with the economy, so he struggled to find a way to goose the growth rate without unleashing inflation. These twin goals, which shaped his economic policies, were in constant tension—and so were the president's advisers. The moderate Kennedy staked out a middle ground, with Secretary of the Treasury C. Douglas Dillon on his right. A Wall Street financier and veteran of the Eisenhower administration, Dillon was appointed to Kennedy's cabinet to appease business leaders leery of a Democrat in the White House. He did battle in favor of free trade and against budget deficits, matching wits with administration liberals like Harvard professor John Kenneth Galbraith, who peppered the president with advice from his far-away post as ambassador to India. Leading the liberals was University of Minnesota economics professor Walter Heller, head of the Council of Economic Advisers. Heller advocated a more active role for government, starting with a Keynesian tax cut to stimulate the economy, coupled with voluntary wage and price controls to dampen inflation. Kennedy's aversion to deficit spending made him worry about the effect a tax cut would have on the budget, but his activist impulse, encouraged by Heller, eventually won out.

As with most of the Kennedy presidency, his economic policy developed gradually. In his first State of the Union message, he sang from the Dillon hymnal, calling for a balanced budget and a stern line against inflation. He promised to continue voluntary wage and price controls, a decision that brought him to the most significant economic clash of his term—a head-on collision with Big Steel in April 1962.

It happened like this: The powerful steelworkers union, urged on by the administration, agreed to accept flat wages and only a modest increase in benefits as part of a new industry-wide contract. Kennedy was delighted by the union's restraint, and although he had no formal arrangement with the manufacturers to keep a lid on prices in return, he assumed they would exercise similar discipline. So he was shocked when Roger Blough, chairman of U.S. Steel, asked for a meeting shortly after the contract was signed and showed up at the White House with a press release announcing a steep price hike. A cold edge in his voice, Kennedy warned Blough that he was "making a mistake," and when other leading steelmakers promptly followed Blough's lead, the president attacked without mercy. Rapidly and ruthlessly, first in private and then in public, the administration pummeled Big Steel. First, Kennedy phoned union leader David McDonald to commiserate. "Dave, you've been screwed and I've been screwed," he said, his Oval Office rocking chair moving furiously. To aides, he seethed, "My father always told me that all businessmen were sons of bitches, but I never believed it till now."

He took to the airwaves. "The simultaneous and identical actions of United States Steel and other leading steel corporations ... constitute a wholly unjustified and irresponsible defiance of the public interest," the president declared. He accused the industry of sapping a billion dollars from the American economy in higher prices, at a time when every penny was needed to fight communism. Firing with every weapon in his arsenal, Kennedy approved as McNamara announced that the Pentagon contract for submarine steel would go to a firm that refused to join in the price hike. At the Justice Department, Robert Kennedy's lawyers opened an antitrust investigation. FBI agents delivered subpoenas to top steel executives, demanding their expense accounts, while other agents fanned out to interview journalists who might have evidence of price-fixing. This immense display of government power brought Big Steel to its knees. With the attorney general prepared to haul industry executives before a grand jury, and the president ready to blame every economic ill on steel prices, Bethlehem Steel capitulated several days after announcing the new price, followed immediately by Blough's U.S. Steel.

Kennedy's face-off with the industry giants won admirers on the left even as he energized his opponents on the right. It helped him survive the growing disenchantment of his liberal supporters over his weak stand on civil rights. But the damage done to his relationship with business was immeasurable. In May, a few weeks after the steel crisis, the stock market fell off a cliff. Worried, the president decided that he must mend fences. He hosted White House dinners and personal photo ops for the titans of American business, but Kennedy's most effective peace offering was his proposal for a major tax cut—which, the liberal Heller assured him, would have the added benefit of fanning economic growth. Although the Kennedy tax cut would not pass until after the president's death, the proposal gave him a record that Republicans extol decades later, delighted to enlist a Democratic hero on the side of lower taxes. In economics, as in so many areas, Kennedy valued pragmatism most of all, and the tax cut appealed to his desire to stimulate spending while mollifying chambers of commerce. As the decades have passed, most historians have praised Kennedy's economic record, though some critics argue that his decisions stacked the fuel that erupted into the runaway inflation of the 1970s.

But even the most adept economic plan could never fire the imagination of Americans as Kennedy's bold commitment to manned spaceflight managed to do. Space was John F. Kennedy at

his best: inspiring and effective at the same time. By setting the goal of putting American boots on the face of the moon before 1970, Kennedy gave the nation a common cause during a period of great division. The surge of federal money and the urgency of the mission gave purpose and momentum to innovations in computing, materials and precision manufacturing—building blocks of the digital revolution. And the space race was flexible response at its most flexible. By opening a peaceful competition in space, Kennedy provided an outlet for superpower rivalry at a time when that rivalry required every possible safe outlet. The race to the moon helped get the world through the perilous 1960s without the catastrophe of direct military confrontation.

It almost didn't happen. Kennedy was a skeptic about manned space travel when he took office. As a senator, he agreed with President Eisenhower that space travel was a waste of money. As president, Kennedy chose for his chief science adviser a noted opponent of human space exploration, Jerome Wiesner, who argued presciently that machines could be designed to do the job more cheaply and more safely. Kennedy was initially reluctant to challenge the Soviets in space because he lacked confidence that the United States could win. "A dictatorship enjoys advantages in this kind of competition," Kennedy observed during his first months in office, because of "its ability to mobilize its resources for a specific purpose." The U.S.S.R. had been the first nation to put a satellite in space and was the first to put a man in orbit. Its rockets in 1961 were the most powerful in the world by far.

Vice President Johnson pushed Kennedy to change his mind. When the president put Johnson in charge of a space task force, the relentless Texan charged ahead. He knew the way to win Kennedy over was to tie events in space to the battle for influence on Earth. Johnson made a strong case that nations around the world would see Soviet achievements in space as evidence of strength, unless the U.S. could first pull even and then pull ahead. "Dramatic accomplishments in space are being increasingly identified as a major indicator of world leadership," he warned in a memo to the president. The U.S. could not surrender in space without paying a heavy price.

LEVELING THE FIELD
The president signed a bill aimed at assuring women equal pay with men for equal work.

When America's leading expert on rocketry, the German engineer Wernher von Braun, assured Kennedy that an intensive effort could yield results within six or seven years, the president was persuaded. In a visionary decision that would become his signature initiative, Kennedy looked at America's sputtering space program and saw past it to the glories of Apollo. His endorsement of the lunar mission, first delivered during a 1961 speech to Congress, drew hearty applause. Soon, though, critics seized on the price tag and asked what better uses could be found for the billions of dollars now earmarked for NASA. By 1962, Kennedy felt obliged to defend his decision, which he did in a ringing speech at Rice University in Texas. A classic example of Kennedy rhetoric, he turned the uncertainty of the future into a test of national mettle. "We choose to go to the moon in this decade ... not because [it is] easy, but because [it is] hard, because that goal will serve to organize and measure the best of our energies and skills," he declared.

Neil Armstrong's first step on the lunar surface seven years after those words were spoken became an instant symbol of America's boundless potential for creative energy when marshaled to a single goal. If we can put a man on the moon, people found themselves asking, what else might we achieve? What earthly problems could be solved through a similar commitment to a common cause? Over the years, the question became a cliché, but the impulse behind it—the very idea and hope of progress—was the best of the Kennedy presidency, distilled to an essence.

HIS FINEST SPEECH

By JEFFREY D. SACHS

IKE ALL NATIONAL LEADERS OF the day, John F. Kennedy was a Cold Warrior, determined to preserve American liberty in the face of the perceived threat of global communism. Yet he was also determined from the first day of his administration to find a path to peace. That path was unclear, and both Kennedy and Soviet leader Nikita Khrushchev would stumble badly along the way, from the Bay of Pigs to the Cuban Missile Crisis. Despite these near disasters, Kennedy and Khrushchev found a way back from the brink and toward a peaceful resolution of the Cold War. JFK's peace campaign found its greatest eloquence during the summer of 1963, notably the great proclamation he delivered as the American University commencement address on June 10, 1963.

The Peace Speech has never achieved the fame of his inaugural address or the great speech on civil rights that he delivered just one day later. I had not really known the speech until I came across it a few years ago while working on issues of global poverty. It moved me deeply, not only for its eloquence and message, but for its relevance to today's global challenges, the most important of which is learning to live together on a crowded Earth. Kennedy noted that the core of our common humanity is that "we all inhabit this small planet. We all breathe the same air." In Kennedy's day the dire threat to the air was nuclear fallout. In our time, it is greenhouse gases. But in both cases the underlying truth is the same: we need to make the planet a fitting home for all of humanity.

The speech he delivered on that June day is a work of magnificent culmination. Kennedy's oratory, backed by the gifted phrases of his counselor and speechwriter Ted Sorensen, was always powerful, but never more so than this speech, where rhetoric, history, leadership and morality converged. To this day, Kennedy's speech stands out as a unique approach to global affairs. Its power derives not just from its bold vision of peace between the U.S. and the Soviet Union but also from its call upon Americans to reexamine their own attitudes toward peace. Kennedy's point was basic yet unusual in international affairs: that there was humanity, decency and valor on both sides of the Cold War divide. And because both sides shared in the same human drama, both would share in the gains from peace. A peace agreement was therefore feasible, because it would be mutually beneficial.

Kennedy knew that he needed the American people on his side. Even if he were to sign a treaty with Khrushchev, it would count for nothing if it died in the Senate. The tragedy of Woodrow Wilson, who succeeded in negotiating the League of Nations only to fail to win Senate ratification for it, was always present in Kennedy's mind. He would need a campaign, Senate vote by Senate vote, to assure the American people that the treaty was in their interest. His success or failure in the peace campaign, he knew, would augur his success or failure in his reelection campaign the following year. And as a campaign begins with a kickoff speech, the campaign for global peace would begin with one as well. There could be no better venue than the hometown university on commencement day.

The speech was prepared by a tight circle of advisers, lest a more skeptical administration member try to derail it or water it down. Sorensen worked on the draft with a few key advisers, including William Foster, the director of the Arms Control and Disarmament Agency. Kennedy was in Hawaii the night before the speech for a meeting of the U.S. Conference of Mayors. Foster recalled the rush to finish: "We worked like hell all day. Then Ted Sorensen, I think, sat up all night with his remarkable ability to polish and write and was able to send each of us and the president the final draft about six or seven in the morning to see if there were changes to be made. We

had another meeting just before the speech, after we got the president's comments back by cable." Sorensen flew to Hawaii to bring the final draft and return with Kennedy on a Sunday night flight, during which Kennedy put his final touches on the address.

Upon landing, Kennedy went briefly to the White House and then straight to the American University campus. The day was sunny and children played on the grass while college students awaited their diplomas. The president rose to the dais to accept an honorary degree and deliver the commencement address. Kennedy quoted the English poet John Masefield, who extolled the university as "a place where those who hate ignorance may strive to know, where those who perceive the truth may strive to make others see." That was Kennedy's task that morning. He would use the occasion to discuss a topic "on which ignorance too often abounds," one he declared to be "the most important topic on earth: world peace." Kennedy defined the challenge in global rather than national terms, the pattern he would follow throughout the 26-minute speech:

What kind of peace do we seek? Not a Pax Americana enforced on the world by American weapons of war. Not the peace of the grave or the security of the slave. I am talking about genuine peace, the kind of peace that makes life on earth worth living, the kind that enables men and nations to grow, and to hope, and build a better life for their children—not merely peace for Americans but peace for all men and women, not merely peace in our time but peace for all time.

Here is the echo of Winston Churchill, who had sought peace "not only for our time, but for a century to come." We also see both men's deliberate contrast with Neville Chamberlain's appeasement at Munich, which he described as "peace for our time."

Next, by explaining the logic of the prisoner's dilemma—how two sides can get trapped in a wasteful and dangerous arms race with both sides ending up the losers—Kennedy showed how peace was possible in a world where war seemed nearly inevitable. First he had to dispel the idea that a nuclear war could be fought and won.

> *Total war makes no sense in an age where great powers can maintain large and relatively invulnerable nuclear forces and refuse to surrender without resort to those forces. It makes no sense in an age where a single nuclear weapon contains almost 10 times the explosive force delivered by all Allied air forces in the Second World War. It makes no sense in an age when the deadly poisons produced by a nuclear exchange would be carried by wind and water and soil and seed to the far corners of the globe and to generations yet unborn.*

Kennedy then acknowledged the perverse logic of deterrence:

> *Today the expenditure of billions of dollars every year on weapons acquired for the purpose of making sure we never need to use them is essential to keeping the peace.*

Yet he rejected the idea that we should be satisfied or comforted by such a situation:

> *But surely the acquisition of such idle stockpiles—which can only destroy and never create—is not the only, much less the most efficient, means of assuring peace.*

For Kennedy knew the arms race was not only hugely costly, but an invitation to a devastating blunder, as had nearly occurred just eight months earlier with the Cuban Missile Crisis. Vast stockpiles of arms in a balance of terror can never deliver the desired security,

at least not in comparison with peace itself. But can peace really be achieved, or is that merely an illusion, a way to be suckered and overtaken by the other side?

Kennedy's answer was that peace is possible despite the many prophets of doom. The barriers are not only in our adversaries but also, remarkably and paradoxically, in ourselves:

> *Some say that it is useless to speak of world peace or world law or world disarmament, and that it will be useless until the leaders of the Soviet Union adopt a more enlightened attitude. I hope they do. I believe we can help them do it. But I also believe that we must reexamine our own attitude, as individuals and as a nation, for our attitude is as essential as theirs.*

Among Kennedy's tasks was to explain why peace should even be considered possible after 18 years of continuous crisis, following six years of devastating war. He began by raising our hopes: that as humans we can solve even our toughest problems.

> *First, let us examine our attitude towards peace itself. Too many of us think it is impossible. Too many think it unreal. But that is a dangerous, defeatist belief. It leads to the conclusion that war is inevitable, that mankind is doomed, that we are gripped by forces we cannot control. We need not accept that view. Our problems are man-made—therefore, they can be solved by man. And man can be as big as he wants. No problem of human destiny is beyond human beings. Man's reason and spirit have often solved the seemingly unsolvable, and we believe they can do it again.*

Yet Kennedy was ever the realist. He quickly cautioned:

> *I am not referring to the absolute, infinite*

*concept of peace and goodwill of which
some fantasies and fanatics dream. I do
not deny the value of hopes and dreams,
but we merely invite discouragement and
incredulity by making that our only and
immediate goal.*

Kennedy invoked his long-held belief that
peace would have to be built step by step:

*Let us focus on a more practical, more
attainable peace, based not on a sudden
revolution in human nature but on a
gradual evolution in human institutions—
on a series of concrete actions and effective
agreements which are in the interest of all
concerned. There is no single, simple key
to this peace, no grand or magic formula to
be adopted by one or two powers. Genuine
peace must be the product of many nations,
the sum of many acts. It must be dynamic,
not static, changing to meet the challenge of
each new generation.*

But how can peace be reached with such
an implacable foe as the Soviet Union? Begin,
Kennedy said, with a realistic assessment of
the conditions for peace:

*World peace, like community peace,
does not require that each man love
his neighbor—it requires only that
they live together in mutual tolerance,
submitting their disputes to a just and
peaceful settlement.*

Moreover, echoing the historian and theo-
rist B.H. Liddell Hart, Kennedy reminded
Americans that:

*history teaches us that enmities between
nations, as between individuals, do not last
forever. However fixed our likes and dislikes
may seem, the tide of time and events will
often bring surprising changes in the*

relations between nations and neighbors.

"So let us persevere," said Kennedy.

Balancing idealism and practicality, the
grand vision of peace with the specific step to
get there, Kennedy charted the way forward
with a lesson in good management that can
serve a thousand purposes:

*By defining our goal more clearly, by
making it seem more manageable and
less remote, we can help all peoples to
see it, to draw hope from it, and to move
irresistibly towards it.*

Here, in one sentence, is the art of great
leadership. Define a goal clearly. Explain how
it can be achieved in manageable steps. Help
others to share the goal—in part through great
oratory. Their hopes will move them "irresistibly" toward the goal.

U.S. foreign policy speeches after World
War II until the Peace Speech often contained
a litany of sins committed by the Soviet Union,
matched by proclamations of America's unerr-
ing and unswerving goodwill. Kennedy sought
to make a very different point. He was not interested in condemning the Soviet Union, in
"piling up debating points," as he put it later
in the speech, but rather in convincing Americans that the Soviet Union shared America's
interests in peace, and so could be a partner in
peace. He started by reminding Americans not
to demonize the Soviet people, however much
Americans might abhor the communist system:

*No government or social system is so
evil that its people must be considered as
lacking in virtue. As Americans, we find
communism profoundly repugnant as a
negation of personal freedom and dignity.
But we can still hail the Russian people for
their many achievements—in science and
space, in economic and industrial growth,
in culture, in acts of courage.*

Peace, Kennedy was emphasizing, requires respect of the other party, a fair and generous appraisal of the other's interests and worth. And Kennedy's praise for the Russians was generous, speaking of their virtue and courage, the classical ideals of citizenship he held highest. Measure by measure, phrase by phrase, Kennedy brilliantly drew America and the Soviet Union into a shared embrace of peace:

Among the many traits the peoples of our two countries have in common, none is stronger than our mutual abhorrence of war. Almost unique among the major world powers, we have never been at war with each other.

Here was a paradox indeed. And Kennedy reminded his listeners of something equally fundamental: the Soviet Union's unmatched sacrifices as the recent ally of the U.S. in the war against Hitler:

And no nation in the history of battle ever suffered more than the Soviet Union suffered in the course of the Second World War. At least 20 million lost their lives. Countless millions of homes and farms were burned or sacked. A third of the nation's territory, including nearly two thirds of its industrial base, was turned into a wasteland—a loss equivalent to the destruction of this country east of Chicago.

But what bound the U.S. and the Soviet Union most in the quest for peace was an irony even stronger than recent history. Though the two countries were the world's strongest, they were also, perversely, the world's most vulnerable. Such was the reality of the nuclear age:

Today, should total war ever break out again—no matter how—our two countries would become the primary targets. It is an ironic but accurate fact that the two strongest powers are the two in the most

danger of devastation. All we have built, all we have worked for, would be destroyed in the first 24 hours.

Kennedy did not stop there, with the devastating tally of a future war, but went on to remind Americans (and Russians) of the crushing costs of the current Cold War itself:

And even in the Cold War, which brings burdens and dangers to so many nations, including this nation's closest allies, our two countries bear the heaviest burdens. For we are both devoting massive sums of money to weapons that could be better devoted to combating ignorance, poverty and disease. We are both caught up in a vicious and dangerous cycle, in which suspicion on one side breeds suspicion on the other, and new weapons beget counterweapons.

Putting together the pieces, the point is clear and overwhelming. Both the U.S. and the Soviet Union abhor war. They have never fought each other. They were allies in the war. They can admire each other's virtue and valor. They risk mutual annihilation. They are squandering their wealth in an arms race. Therefore, they also share a common interest in peace. In reaching this conclusion, Kennedy's rhetoric soared with empathy and insight, in what to my mind are the most eloquent and important words of the speech, and perhaps of his presidency:

So let us not be blind to our differences, but let us also direct attention to our common interests and the means by which those differences can be resolved. And if we cannot end now our differences, at least we can help make the world safe for diversity. For, in the final analysis, our most basic common link is that we all inhabit this small planet. We all breathe the same air. We all cherish our children's futures. And we are all mortal.

Kennedy was not yet done batting down the preconceptions and myths that held the world at the brink of the abyss. He enjoined the world to learn the lessons of the Cold War and the harrowing Cuban Missile Crisis. As he had remarked soon after the crisis, we can't go on living this way. The Cold War could too easily become a hot war. We must comport ourselves on both sides to avoid disaster, he urged, warning of the dangers of pushing foes to the point of war or humiliating retreat:

Above all, while defending our own vital interests, nuclear powers must avert those confrontations which bring an adversary to a choice of either a humiliating retreat or a nuclear war. To adopt that kind of course in the nuclear age would be evidence only of the bankruptcy of our policy—or of a collective death wish for the world.

Kennedy was teaching about the dangerous dynamics of crises. These are not just about power, military might and strategic calculations. They are about pride and humiliation. Any leader must put himself in the position of his counterpart, to understand the implications of his or her own actions for the other side—in human, psychological and social terms.

Kennedy called for a resumption of disarmament talks, implicitly returning to the timetable he had proposed at the U.N. General Assembly in 1961:

Our primary long-range interest ... is general and complete disarmament, designed to take place by stages, permitting parallel political developments to build the new institutions of peace which would take the place of arms.

Kennedy's primary focus in these disarmament talks would be a nuclear test-ban treaty, which he emphasized for several reasons: widespread public concern over nuclear fallout from the tests, which had steadily grown since several Japanese fishermen died from fallout poisoning after a U.S nuclear test in 1954; a hope that a test ban would slow proliferation, notably to China; a belief among scientists that weapons design could proceed even without the tests; and an overarching hope that an agreement on tests would create the momentum for further agreements.

Kennedy concluded the Peace Speech with two important announcements. The first was that Khrushchev, Kennedy and British prime minister Harold Macmillan, the leaders of the three nuclear powers, had just agreed to talks in Moscow to try to complete a test-ban treaty. The second was a matter of goodwill, that the U.S. would not conduct nuclear tests as long as other states did not do so. Both announcements were interrupted by the vigorous applause of those gathered. The listeners that morning recognized that something new and important was getting under way. And indeed it was. By the end of the following month, the Partial Nuclear Test Ban Treaty was signed in Moscow, and by September it was ratified by the U.S. Senate.

Now it is our turn. We still threaten ourselves with our own destruction. We know that our tasks are large; so too are the acts of past leadership that inspire us and encourage us on our way. We have been granted the lessons of John Kennedy's peace initiative, and the gift of his and Ted Sorensen's words for our age and beyond. We are not gripped by forces beyond our control. We too can be as big as we want. We too can take our stand and move the world.

Jeffrey Sachs is director of the Earth Institute at Columbia University and Special Adviser to U.N. Secretary General Ban Ki-moon.

CHAPTER FIVE

ELEVATED BY
HIS DEATH

⌄

WARMED BY THE CROWD
*Despite ill political winds in
Texas, the Kennedys were
greeted that day in Dallas by
cheering throngs.*

By DAVID VON DREHLE
Photographs by H. WARNER KING

IN 1962, HARVARD HISTORIAN ARTHUR SCHLESINGER—THE FATHER OF KENNEDY'S AIDE AND CHRONICLER OF THE SAME NAME—REPEATED A FAMOUS SURVEY HE HAD CONDUCTED AFTER WORLD WAR II, IN WHICH HE ASKED HISTORIANS TO

rank the presidents in order of greatness. When the results were published, Lincoln, Washington and Franklin D. Roosevelt were once again at the top of the list, with Harding, Grant and Buchanan once again in the cellar. Around this time, John F. Kennedy had a visit from another historian, David Herbert Donald, who listened as the incumbent complained bitterly about the scrutiny that he knew would someday be turned on him, too. "No one has a right to grade a president—even poor James Buchanan—who has not sat in his chair, examined the mail and information that came across his desk, and learned why he made his decisions," Kennedy said.

But the compulsion to rate presidents has only spread in the years since the Schlesinger survey, and if Kennedy had realized how kindly the judges would look on his record, perhaps he would not have been so harsh. Of all the presidents who served less than one full term, he gets by far the highest marks. Indeed, a 2009 C-SPAN survey of historians and other experts ranked Kennedy among the top 10 presidents overall. He fares even better with the general public, typically commanding one of the top five spots when ordinary citizens are doing the voting.

Kennedy's reputation glows despite revelations of the extreme recklessness with which he conducted his personal life. His sexual conquests as president ranged from a teenage intern to the wife of a friend and associate. He was both exhibitionist and voyeur during afternoon orgies in the White House swimming pool. Secret Service agents tried in vain to keep track of the stream of unknown women, including some prostitutes, who were ushered past the guards to meet with the president. In one notorious case, Kennedy shared a mistress with Chicago mob boss Sam Giancana—both men were introduced to Judith Campbell Exner by their mutual friend Frank Sinatra. Giancana had been recruited at the time to help the CIA kill Castro. When FBI director J. Edgar Hoover, a man despised by the Kennedys, uncovered the unseemly triangle, he paid a call on the president to warn him of the danger of blackmail. Hoover, who knew a thing or two about blackmail, left the Oval Office that day confident that the Kennedys would pose no threat to his job security.

Kennedy's licentious behavior deeply wounded his young wife Jacqueline, whose beauty and poise were essential to his calculatedly misleading image as head of America's most glamorous family. Those close to the family wondered whether their marriage could survive Jackie Kennedy's feelings of humiliation. And when his sexual excesses are added to his extensive drug use (interrelated matters, given the effect of steroids and amphetamines on libido), it is clear that John F. Kennedy teetered on a precipice in his personal life even as he stared into the abyss as a world leader.

His reputation had survived those tawdry details for the simple fact that he was lifted far beyond them by the shocking suddenness of his death. In similar fashion, his death elevated him above the wrenching upheaval of the new world he had helped to make. Through riots, protests and proxy wars around the globe, beleaguered presidents from Lyndon Johnson to Barack Obama have labored with the ghost of Kennedy hovering over them, an eternally charismatic what-if. The assassination burned away the flaws and rough edges of the Kennedy presidency while heightening his best qualities: "That lightsome tread, that debonair touch, that shock of chestnut hair, that beguiling grin, that shattering understatement—these are what we shall remember," the insightful columnist Mary McGrory wrote after his death.

Inevitably, Kennedy's presidency was something less than the full embodiment of his dazzling first day in office. But the gap between the promise and the reality has been bridged by the sense of what might have been. All the good that flowed through the years after his death can be credited to his inspiration, while the bad—Vietnam, campus unrest, race riots—is charged to the accounts of others. Death has been called the great leveler, but an exceptional few are exalted by it. John F. Kennedy has been one of those few.

In a humble yet crucial way, however, the Kennedy presidency was also something more than anyone imagined when it began. It was a vindication of the promise that presidents can grow into the job, as all of them must do. Kennedy grew not as a demigod, from strength to strength. He grew as mere mortals grow: by listening, watching, and learning from his many mistakes. John F. Kennedy was wrong about a number of things, and late to get other things right. Ultimately, though, he found his way to the right side of the questions that mattered most. He concluded that nuclear war must never be fought, and is best avoided through strength. He realized that equality deferred is equality denied. And perhaps most of all, he came to see that America's strength lies in its capacity to take on a difficult challenge, and its willingness to do so whenever a true leader points the way.

Kennedy's well-wishers crowded close to his limousine as the motorcade moved toward Dealey Plaza.

HIS LEGACY

What JFK meant to me: a gallery of reflections

"HIS WORDS NEVER FAIL TO INSPIRE. HE PUT HIS FINGER ON THE LIVING PULSE OF OUR COUNTRY."

YO-YO MA, cellist

"The Cuban Missile Crisis was the defining moment of that generation up to that point. His handling of it on the public stage was so dramatic that it served as a catharsis for the near-death experience being faced by the entire nation."

MATTHEW WEINER, creator, *Mad Men*

"WITH ALL HIS HEART, HE ADVOCATED FOR A CITIZENRY THAT CARED FOR, INVESTED AND ENGAGED IN THE COUNTRY THEY WERE LUCKY TO CALL HOME. TO THIS DAY, WE ARE BETTER AND STRONGER BECAUSE OF IT."

JOSEPH P. KENNEDY III, U.S. Representative for Massachusetts

"The work of all the Kennedy brothers very much influenced my decision to vote Democratic when I became a citizen. I think the family's work for the poor and the needy will be remembered for many centuries."

MIKHAIL BARYSHNIKOV, dancer and artistic director

"NEITHER SAINT NOR SUPERMAN, KENNEDY WAS STILL OUR MOST CHARISMATIC PRESIDENT. MANY HAVE TRIED TO IMITATE HIM, BUT HE HAS NOT BEEN REPLACED."

MADELEINE ALBRIGHT, former U.S. Secretary of State

"HE LED WITH HIS EYE ON THE HORIZON, NOT JUST THE NEXT ELECTION. MY GENERATION AROUND THE WORLD IS THE BETTER FOR IT."

DEVAL PATRICK, Massachusetts governor

"HE USHERED IN A SENSE OF HOPE, A SENSE OF OPTIMISM. HE GAVE US THE SENSE THAT WE COULD DO THINGS, WE COULD TRAVEL A DISTANCE."

JOHN LEWIS, civil rights leader and U.S. Representative for Georgia

"As the leader of this great nation, he stood firm and determined in a most profound and memorable way and continues to infuse that spirit of courage into the heart and soul of America."

SIDNEY POITIER, actor

"THE CENTRAL THEMES OF *CAMELOT* WERE ABOUT HOPE, HONOR, HUMANITY AND PEACE. I BELIEVE PRESIDENT KENNEDY EMBRACED THESE IDEALS."

JULIE ANDREWS, actor and singer

"I met President Kennedy in 1962. It was a transformative moment. I was hit with this sense that public service is what I ought to be doing, and that politics itself was a noble undertaking."

JOHN KERRY, U.S. Secretary of State

"President Kennedy imbued in us a greater sense of optimism and self-belief, where Ireland could look confidently to its future with a strong sense of our place in the world."

ENDA KENNY, Prime Minister of Ireland

"For this fiddle player, one of his most enduring legacies will be his commitment to excellence in the arts and his recognition that a civilization is in large part measured by its culture."

ITZHAK PERLMAN, violinist and conductor

"HE GAVE ME OPTIMISM THAT ONE PERSON COULD MAKE A DIFFERENCE; THAT OUR COLLECTIVE INDIVIDUALISM COULD CHANGE THE WORLD."

FRANK GEHRY, architect

"I grew up at a time when if you went inside a black church, you would see a picture of Dr. King, Bobby Kennedy and JFK on the wall in church, like they were part of Jesus's crew. You wanted to be like them, aspire to give to the country what they gave to the country."

VAN JONES, president, Rebuild the Dream

"HE WAS A MAN OF GREAT CURIOSITY. WHEN I BRIEFED HIM ON PLANS FOR PROJECT MERCURY, OUR FIRST ORBITAL FLIGHT, HE ASKED SO MANY QUESTIONS THAT I VOLUNTEERED TO RETURN FOR A SECOND VISIT, THIS TIME WITH MODELS, DIAGRAMS AND MOCK-UPS."

JOHN GLENN, former U.S. Marine Corps pilot, astronaut and U.S. senator

"OVER 40 YEARS AGO, WHEN I ARRIVED IN THE DOMINICAN REPUBLIC, I WAS ASKED A QUESTION I'VE BEEN ASKED A THOUSAND TIMES SINCE: 'WHY DID YOU JOIN THE PEACE CORPS?' THE ANSWER WAS SIMPLE: BECAUSE AN AMERICAN PRESIDENT ASKED ME TO."

CHRIS DODD, former U.S. senator

"All subsequent presidents have used many of the tools Kennedy effortlessly pioneered to connect with the public's imagination. Bill Clinton co-opted that JFK gaze in many of his official photographs: eyes looking off-camera and slightly above, to a bright future on the horizon."

ROB LOWE, actor, playing the role of JFK in the forthcoming *Killing Kennedy*

"KENNEDY VERY EFFECTIVELY USHERED THE WWII GENERATION—WHICH HAD FOUGHT TO DEFEND AMERICA IN ITS DARKEST HOUR—FROM A ROLE OF SERVICE INTO ONE OF GOVERNANCE."

BOB DOLE, former U.S. senator

"My father coached at Navy, and President Kennedy had a passion for football and a well-documented affinity for that team and its players. I attended the Army-Navy game under very tragic, very surreal and emotional circumstances one week after the assassination. That day, Navy stopped Army at the two-yard line on the game's final play for a 21-15 victory. I learned life lessons on leadership, teamwork and mental toughness from being around that team, also known as the President's Team."

BILL BELICHICK, head coach, New England Patriots

"As a young artist at the time, I was moved by his words about the sometimes controversial role of the artist in society: '[The artist] must often sail against the currents of his time. This is not a popular role.' Being criticized myself for speaking out, his words encouraged me to continue to do so."

BARBRA STREISAND, singer, actor and director

CREDITS

∨

ABOUT THE AUTHOR

David Von Drehle is a TIME editor-at-large, former assistant managing editor for the *Washington Post* and author of *Rise to Greatness: Abraham Lincoln and America's Most Perilous Year* as well as three other books, including *Triangle: The Fire That Changed America*.

EXCLUSIVE PHOTOS

The three never-before-published photographs in Chapter Five were made by H. Warner King, a salesman for a jewelry manufacturer, as he watched the president's motorcade in Dallas on Nov. 22, 1963. In storage for nearly half a century, the pictures were recently rediscovered by King's daughter, Sonia. Taken with a Leica camera on Kodachrome slide film, they chronicle the final minutes of Kennedy's life as the presidential limousine traveled along Lemmon Avenue toward Dealey Plaza.

TIME

Managing Editor Richard Stengel
Design Director D.W. Pine
Director of Photography Kira Pollack

JFK: His Enduring Legacy

Editor Stephen Koepp
Designer D.W. Pine
Photo Editor Liz Ronk
Writers David Von Drehle, Ben Cosgrove, Michael Duffy, Nancy Gibbs, Daniel S. Levy, Chris Matthews, Jeffrey D. Sachs
Reporters Melissa August, Lena Finkel, Mary Hart
Graphics Skye Gurney
Editorial Production Lionel P. Vargas

Time Home Entertainment

Publisher Jim Childs
Vice President, Brand & Digital Strategy Steven Sandonato
Executive Director, Marketing Services Carol Pittard
Executive Director, Retail & Special Sales Tom Mifsud
Executive Publishing Director Joy Butts
Director, Bookazine Development & Marketing Laura Adam
Finance Director Glenn Buonocore
Associate Publishing Director Megan Pearlman
Associate General Counsel Helen Wan
Assistant Director, Special Sales Ilene Schreider
Brand Manager Bryan Christian
Associate Production Manager Kimberly Marshall
Associate Brand Manager Isata Yansaneh
Associate Prepress Manager Alex Voznesenskiy

Editorial Director Stephen Koepp
Copy Chief Rina Bander
Design Manager Anne-Michelle Gallero

Special Thanks Katherine Barnet, Jeremy Biloon, Susan Chodakiewicz, Rose Cirrincione, Jacqueline Fitzgerald, Christine Font, Diane Francis, Jenna Goldberg, Hillary Hirsch, David Kahn, Amy Mangus, Nina Mistry, Dave Rozzelle, Ricardo Santiago, Gina Scauzillo, Adriana Tierno, Time Inc. Premedia, TIME Research Center, Vanessa Wu

Copyright © 2013 Time Home Entertainment Inc.
Published by Time Books, an imprint of Time Home Entertainment Inc.
135 West 50th Street, New York, NY 10020

ISBN 10: 1-61893-085-0
ISBN 13: 978-1-61893-085-9
Library of Congress control number: 2013946394

We welcome your comments and suggestions about TIME Books. Please write to us at: TIME Books, Attention: Book Editors, P.O. Box 11016, Des Moines, IA 50336-1016. If you would like to order any of our hardcover Collector's Edition books, please call us at 1-800-327-6388, Monday through Friday, 7 a.m. to 8 p.m., or Saturday, 7 a.m. to 6 p.m., Central Time.